FRENCH
PHRASEBOOK

English edition prepared by First Edition Translations.
Additional phrases provided by Quarto Translations.

Produced by AA Publishing
First published in 1995 as Wat & Hoe Frans,
© Kosmos Uitgevers – Utrecht/Antwerpen

Fifth edition © AA Media Limited 2023
First published 1997

A CIP catalogue record for this book is available from the British Library.

Published by AA Media Limited, whose registered office is Grove House,
Lutyens Close, Basingstoke, Hants, RG24 8AG. Registered number
06112600.

Printed and bound in China by 1010 Printing International Limited

ISBN 978-0-7495-8363-7

A05858

Contents

1   Useful lists 14–28

2   Courtesies 29–38

3   Conversation 39–53

4   Eating out 54–68

Introduction

● **Welcome to the AA's French phrasebook**.

Key sections

This book is divided into 15 themed sections and starts with a
pronunciation table (see opposite), which gives you the phonetic
spelling to all the words and phrases you'll need to know for your trip,
This is followed by a **grammar guide** (page 9), which will help you
construct basic sentences in your chosen language. At the back of the
book (page 167 onwards), you'll find an extensive **word list**.

Finding the right phrase

Throughout the book you'll come across boxes featuring a ☛ symbol
These are designed to help you if you can't understand what your
listener is saying to you. Hand the book over to them and encourage
them to point to the appropriate answer to the question you are asking

Other tinted boxes in the book – this time without the symbol – give
alphabetical listings of themed words with their English translations
beside them.

For extra clarity, we have put all English words and phrases in black,
foreign language terms in colour and phonetic pronunciations in italic.

Enjoy your trip

This phrasebook covers all the subjects you are likely to encounter
during the course of your visit, from reserving a room for the night to
ordering food and drink and what to do if your car breaks down or you
lose your money. With over 2,000 commonly used words and phrases
at your fingertips, you'll be able to get by in all situations. Let this book
become your passport to a secure and enjoyable trip.

Pronunciation table

The pronunciation provided should be read as if it were English, bearing in mind the following main points:

Vowels

a, à or â	a in man	ah	table	tahbl
é	like a in make	ay	été	aytay
è, ê, e	like ai in air	eh	rêve	rehv
e	sometimes	uh	le, ne, je, me	luh, nuh, jhuh, muh
	like u in fluff			
i	like ee in seen	ee	si	see
ô	like o in foam	oa	hôtel	oatehl
o	like o in John	o	homme	om
	sometimes like ô	oa	arroser	ahroasay
u	between ee and ew	ew	tu	tew

Combinations of letters which represent vowel sounds:

ez, er	similar to é	ay	louer	looay
ais, ait	the eh sound	eh	fait	feh
au, eau	similar to ô	oa	beau	boa
ail	like i in side	ahy	travail	trahvahy
ei	similar to è	eh	Seine	sehn
eille	eh + y as in yes	ehy	bouteille	bootehy
eu	similar to e above	uh	feu	fuh
iè	ye as in yes	yeh	siècle	syehkl
ié, ier, iez	y + the ay sound	yay	janvier	jhohnvyay
ille	ee + y as in yes	eey	famille	fameey
oi, oy	combines w + a	wah	moi	mwah
ou, oû	oo as in hoot	oo	vous	voo
ui	combines w and ee	wee	cuir	kweer

Consonants

ch	like **sh** in **sh**ine	*sh*	**chaud**	*shoa*
ç	like **s** in **s**ome	*s*	**garçon**	*gahrsawn*
g	before **e**, **i** and **y**			
	like **s** in lei**s**ure	*jh*	**nager**	*nahjhay*
	before **a**, **o** and **u**			
	like **g** in **g**ot	*g*	**gâteau**	*gahtoa*
gn	like **ny** in ca**ny**on	*ny*	**agneau**	*ahnyoa*
h	silent			
j	like **s** in lei**s**ure	*jh*	**jour**	*jhoor*
qu	like **k** in **k**ind	*k*	**que**	*kuh*
r	rolled at the back of the throat			
w	like **v** in **v**ine	*v*	**wagonlit**	*vahgawnlee*

Nasal sounds

Nasal sounds are written in French by adding an n to a vowel or a combination of vowels pronounced as the English ng:

an/am, **en/em**	a little like **song**	*ohn*	**français**, **lentement**	*frohnseh*, *lohntmohn*
in/im, **ain**, **aim**, **ein**	a little like **bang**	*ahn*	**instant**, **faim**	*ahnstohn*, *fahn*
on/om	a nasal form of **awn**	*awn*	**non**	*nawn*
un/um	a little like **rung**	*uhn*	**un**	*uhn*
ien	**y** + the **ahn** sound	*yahn*	**bien**	*byahn*

Basic grammar

1 The article

French nouns are divided into 2 categories: masculine and feminine. The definite article (the) is **le**, **la** or **l'**:

le is used before masculine words starting with a consonant, **le magasin** (the shop)

la is used with feminine words starting with a consonant, **la plage** (the beach)

l' is used before masculine and feminine words starting with a vowel, **l'argent** (the money), **l'assiette** (the plate).

Other examples are:

le toit   the roof
la maison   the house
l'hôtel (m.)   the hotel
l'entrée (f.)   the entrance

In the case of the indefinite article (**a**, **an**):

un is used before masculine words, **un livre** (a book)

une is used before feminine words, **une pomme** (an apple)

des is used before plural words, both masculine and feminine, **des camions** (lorries), **des voitures** (cars).

Other examples are:

un père	a father	**une mère**	a mother
un homme	a man	**une femme**	a woman
des hommes	men	**des femmes**	women

2 The plural

The plural of **le**, **la** and **l'** is **les**.
The plural of most French nouns ends in **s**, but this **s** is not pronounced. However when the noun begins with a vowel or a silent **h**, then the **s** of **les** or **des** is pronounced **z**, **les affaires** (layzahfehr), **des enfants** (dayzohngfohn).

Other examples are:

le lit	luh lee	**les lits**	lay lee
la table	lah tahbl	**les tables**	lay tahbl
l'avion (m.)	lahveeawn	**les avions**	layzahvyeeawn
l'heure (f.	luhr	**les heures**	layzuhr

Certain plurals end in **aux** (mainly words ending in '**al**')

le cheval	**les chevaux**
le canal	**les canaux**

3 Personal pronouns

I	**je**
You	**tu**
He/she/it	**il/elle**
We	**nous**
You	**vous**
They	**ils/elles**

In general 'tu' is used to translate 'you' when speaking to close friends, relatives and children. **Vous** is used in all other cases. '**It**' becomes **il** or **elle** according to whether the noun referred to is masculine or feminine.

4 Possessive pronouns

	masculine	feminine	plural
my	**mon**	**ma**	**mes**
your	**ton**	**ta**	**tes**
his/her/its	**son**	**sa**	**ses**
our	**notre**	**notre**	**nos**
your	**votre**	**votre**	**vos**
their	**leur**	**leur**	**leurs**

They agree with the object they refer to, e.g. her hat = **son chapeau**.

5 Verbs

parler		to speak
je parle	root + -e	I speak
tu parles	root + -es	you speak
il/elle parle	root + -e	he/she/it speaks
nous parlons	root + -ons	we speak
vous parlez	root + -ez	you speak
ils/elles parlent	root + -ent	they speak
parlé (past participle)		spoken

Here are some useful verbs.

être	to be
je suis	I am
tu es	you are
il/elle est	he/she/it is

11

nous sommes	we are
vous êtes	you are
ils/elles sont	they are
été (past participle)	been
avoir	to have
j'ai	I have
tu as	you have
il/elle a	he/she/it has
nous avons	we have
vous avez	you have
ils/elles ont	they have
eu (past participle)	had
faire	to do/make
je fais	I do
tu fais	you do
il/elle fait	he/she does
nous faisons	we do
vous faites	you do
ils/elles font	they do
fait (past participle)	done/made

6 Countries and prepositions

Names of countries take the article:

L'Angleterre	England
Le Canada	Canada
La France	France
in Paris	**à Paris**
in France	**en France**
in Canada	**au Canada**

7 Negatives

Negatives are formed by using:

ne (verb) **pas**	not
ne (verb) **jamais**	never

Je ne parle pas français.	I don't speak French.
Je ne fume jamais.	I never smoke.

1. Useful lists

What day is it today?	C'est quel jour aujourd'hui?
	seh kehl jhoor oajhoordwee?
Today's Monday.	Aujourd'hui c'est lundi.
	oajhoordwee seh luhndee
– Tuesday.	Aujourd'hui c'est mardi.
	oajhoordwee seh mahrdee
– Wednesday.	Aujourd'hui c'est mercredi.
	oajhoordwee seh mehrkruhdee
– Thursday.	Aujourd'hui c'est jeudi.
	oajhoordwee seh jhuhdee
– Friday.	Aujourd'hui c'est vendredi.
	oajhoordwee seh vohndruhdee
– Saturday.	Aujourd'hui c'est samedi.
	oajhoordwee seh sahmdee
– Sunday.	Aujourd'hui c'est dimanche.
	oajhoordwee seh deemohnsh
in January	en janvier
	ohn jhohnvyay
since February	depuis février
	duhpwee fayvryay
in spring	au printemps
	oa prahntohn
in summer	en été; l'été
	ohn naytay; laytay
in autumn	en automne
	ohn noatonn
in winter	en hiver; l'hiver
	ohn neevehr; leevehr
the 21st century	le 21ème siècle
	luh vahnt ay ewn yehm seeehcl
What's the date today?	Quelle est la date aujourd'hui?
	kehl eh lah daht oajhoordwee?
Today's the 24th.	Aujourd'hui on est le vingt-quatre.
	oajhoordwee awn neh luh vahnkahtr

Tomorrow is...	Demain c'est... *duhmahn say*
Monday 3 July 2023	lundi, le trois juillet 2023 *luhndee, luh trwah jhweeyeh duh meel vahn trwah*
in the morning	le matin *luh mahtahn*
in the afternoon	l'après-midi *lahpreh meedee*
in the evening	le soir *luh swahr*
at night	la nuit *lah nwee*
this morning	ce matin *suh mahtahn*
this afternoon	cet après-midi *seht ahpreh meedee*
this evening	ce soir *suh swahr*
tonight	ce soir *suh swahr*
last night	hier soir *yehr swahr*
this week	cette semaine *seht suhmehn*
next month	le mois prochain *luh mwah proshahn*
last year	l'année passée *lahnay pahsay*
next...	prochain/prochaine *proshahn/proshehn*
in...days/weeks/ months/years	dans...jours/semaines/mois/ans *dohn...jhoor/suhmehn/mwah/ohn*
...weeks ago	il y a...semaines *eel ee ah...suhmehn*
day off	jour de congé *jhoor duh kawnjhay*

1.2 Bank holidays

● The most important Bank holidays in France are the following:

January 1	Le Jour de l'An (New Year's Day)
March/April	Pâques, (Easter)
	le lundi de Pâques (Easter Monday)
May 1	La Fête du Travail (May Day; Labour Day)
May 8	Le Jour de la Libération (Liberation Day)
May/June	L'Ascension; la Pentecôte (Ascension; Whit Sunday)
July 14	La Fête Nationale (Bastille Day)
August 15	L'Assomption (Assumption)
November 1	La Toussaint (All Saints' Day)
November 11	L'Armistice (Armistice Day)
December 25	Noël (Christmas)

Most shops, banks and government institutions are closed on these days. Banks close the afternoon before a Bank holiday and some banks close on Mondays in the provinces. Good Friday and Boxing Day are not Bank Holidays

1.3 What time is it?

What time is it?	Quelle heure est-il?
	kehl uhr eh teel?
It's nine o'clock.	Il est neuf heures.
	eel eh nuh vuhr
- five past ten.	Il est dix heures cinq.
	eel eh dee zuhr sahnk
- a quarter past eleven.	Il est onze heures et quart.
	eel eh tawnz uhr ay kahr
- twenty past twelve.	Il est douze heures vingt.
	eel eh dooz uhr vahn
- half past one.	Il est une heure et demie.
	eel eh tewn uhr ay duhmee

– twenty–five to three.	Il est trois heures moins vingt-cinq.
	eel eh trwah zuhr mwahn vahn sahnk
– a quarter to four.	Il est quatre heures moins le quart.
	eel eh kahtr uhr mwahn luh kahr
– ten to five.	Il est cinq heures moins dix.
	eel eh sahnk uhr mwahn dees
– twelve noon.	Il est midi.
	eel eh meedee
– midnight.	Il est minuit.
	eel eh meenwee
half an hour	une demi-heure
	ewn duhmee uhr
What time?	A quelle heure?
	ah kehl uhr?
What time can I come round?	A quelle heure puis-je venir?
	ah kehl uhr pwee jhuh vuhneer?
At...	A...
	ah...
After...	Après...
	ahpreh...
Before...	Avant...
	ahvohn...
Between...and...	Entre...et...
	ohntr...ay...
From...to...	De...à...
	duh...ah...
In...minutes.	Dans...minutes.
	dohn...meenewt
– an hour.	Dans une heure.
	dohn zewn uhr
– ...hours.	Dans...heures.
	dohn...uhr
– a quarter of an hour.	Dans un quart d'heure.
	dohn zuhn kahr duhr
– three quarters of an hour.	Dans trois quarts d'heure.
	dohn trwah kahr duhr

early/late	trop tôt/tard
	troa toa/tahr
on time	à temps
	ah tohn
summertime	l'heure d'été
	luhr daytay
wintertime	l'heure d'hiver
	luhr deevehr

1.4 One, two, three...

0	zéro	*zayroa*
1	un	*uhn*
2	deux	*duh*
3	trois	*trwah*
4	quatre	*kahtr*
5	cinq	*sahnk*
6	six	*sees*
7	sept	*seht*
8	huit	*weet*
9	neuf	*nuhf*
10	dix	*dees*
11	onze	*awnz*
12	douze	*dooz*
13	treize	*trehz*
14	quatorze	*kahtorz*
15	quinze	*kahnz*
16	seize	*sehz*
17	dix-sept	*dee seht*
18	dix-huit	*dee zweet*
19	dix-neuf	*deez nuhf*
20	vingt	*vahn*
21	vingt et un	*vahn tay uhn*
22	vingt-deux	*vahn duh*

30	trente	*trohnt*
31	trente et un	*trohn tay uhn*
32	trente-deux	*trohnt duh*
40	quarante	*kahrohnt*
50	cinquante	*sahnkohnt*
60	soixante	*swahssohnt*
70	soixante-dix	*swahssohnt dees*
80	quatre-vingts	*kahtr vahn*
90	quatre-vingt-dix	*kahtr vahn dees*
100	cent	*sohn*
101	cent un	*sohn uhn*
110	cent dix	*sohn dees*
120	cent vingt	*sohn vahn*
200	deux cents	*duh sohn*
300	trois cents	*trwah sohn*
400	quatre cents	*kahtr sohn*
500	cinq cents	*sahnk sohn*
600	six cents	*see sohn*
700	sept cents	*seht sohn*
800	huit cents	*wee sohn*
900	neuf cents	*nuhf sohn*
1,000	mille	*meel*
1,100	mille cent	*meel sohn*
2,000	deux mille	*duh meel*
10,000	dix mille	*dee meel*
100,000	cent mille	*sohn meel*
1,000,000	un million	*uhn meelyawn*
1st	le premier	*luh pruhmyay*
2nd	le deuxième	*luh duhzyehm*
3rd	le troisième	*luh trwahzyehm*
4th	le quatrième	*luh kahtryehm*
5th	le cinquième	*luh sahnkyehm*
6th	le sixième	*luh seezyehm*
7th	le septième	*luh sehtyehm*
8th	le huitième	*luh weetyehm*

9th	le neuvième	*luh nuhvyehm*
10th	le dixième	*luh deezyehm*
11th	le onzième	*luh awnzyehm*
12th	le douzième	*luh doozyehm*
13th	le treizième	*luh trehzyehm*
14th	le quatorzième	*luh kahtorzyehm*
15th	le quinzième	*luh kahnzyehm*
16th	le seizième	*luh sehzyehm*
17th	le dix-septième	*luh dee sehtyehm*
18th	le dix-huitième	*luh dee zweetyehm*
19th	le dix-neuvième	*luh deez nuhvyehm*
20th	le vingtième	*luh vahntyehm*
21st	le vingt et unième	*luh vahn tay-ewnyehm*
22nd	le vingt-deuxième	*luh vahn duhzyehm*
30th	le trentième	*luh trohntyehm*
100th	le centième	*luh sohntyehm*
1,000th	le millième	*luh meelyehm*
once	une fois	*ewn fwah*
twice	deux fois	*duh fwah*
double	le double	*luh doobl*
triple	le triple	*luh treepl*
half	la moitié	*lah mwahtyay*
a quarter	un quart	*uhn kahr*
a third	un tiers	*uhn tyehr*

a couple, a few, some   quelques, un nombre de, quelques
kehlkuh, uhn nawnbr duh, kehlkuh

odd/even   impair/pair
ahnpehr/pehr

total   (au) total
(oa) totahl

1.5 The weather

Is the weather going to be good/bad?	Va-t-il faire beau/mauvais?
	vah teel fehr boa/moaveh?
Is it going to get colder/hotter?	Va-t-il faire plus froid/plus chaud?
	vah teel fehr plew frwah/plew shoa?
What temperature is it going to be?	Quelle température va-t-il faire?
	Kehl tohnpayrahtewr vah teel fehr?
Is it going to rain?	Va-t-il pleuvoir?
	vah teel pluhvwahr?
Is there going to be a storm?	Va-t-il faire de la tempête?
	vah teel fehr duh lah tohnpeht?
Is it going to snow?	Va-t-il neiger?
	vah teel nehjhay?
Is it going to freeze?	Va-t-il geler?
	vah teel jhuhlay?
Is the thaw setting in?	Va-t-il dégeler?
	vah teel dayjhuhlay?
Is it going to be foggy?	Y aura-t-il du brouillard?
	ee oarah teel dew brooy-yahr?
Is there going to be a thunderstorm?	Va-t-il faire de l'orage?
	vah teel fehr duh lorahjh?
The weather's changing.	Le temps change.
	luh tohn shohnjh
It's cooling down.	Ça se rafraîchit.
	sah suh rahfrehshee
What's the weather going to be like today/tomorrow?	Quel temps va-t-il faire aujour d'hui/demain?
	kehl tohn vah teel fehr oajhoordwee/ duhmahn?

nuageux	**pluvieux**	**les rafales de vent**
cloudy	raining	squalls
beau	**la canicule**	**l'ouragan (m.)**
fine	scorching hot	hurricane
chaud	**la grêle**	**lourd**
hot	hail	muggy
...degrés	**la neige**	**l'orage (m.)**
(au-dessous/au-	snow	thunderstorm
dessus de zéro)	**la pluie**	**orageux**
...degrees (below/	rain	stormy
above zero)	**la vague de chaleur**	**pénétrant**
couvert	heatwave	bleak
overcast	**l'averse (f.)**	**ciel dégagé**
le crachin	shower	clear
drizzle	**le brouillard**	**brumeux**
doux	fog	misty
mild	**le gel**	**vent faible/**
ensoleillé	ice	**modéré/fort**
sunny	**le vent**	light/moderate/
frais	wind	strong wind
chilly	**le verglas**	**venteux**
froid	black ice	windy
cold	**les nuages**	
humide	clouds	
damp		

1.6 Here, there...

See also **5.1 Asking for directions**

here/there	ici/là
	eesee/lah
somewhere/nowhere	quelque part/nulle part
	kehlkuh pahr/newl pahr
everywhere	partout
	pahrtoo
far away/nearby	loin/à côté
	lwahn/ah koatay
right/left	la droite/la gauche
	lah drwaht/lah goash
to the right/left of	à droite de/à gauche de
	ah drwaht duh/ah goash duh
straight ahead	tout droit
	too drwah
via	par
	pahr
in	dans
	dohn
on	sur
	sewr
under	sous
	soo
against	contre
	kawntr
opposite	en face de
	ohn fahs duh
next to	à côté de
	ah koatay duh
near	près de
	preh duh
in front of	devant
	devohn

in the centre	au milieu de
	oa meelyuh duh
forward	en avant
	ohn nahvohn
down	en bas
	ohn bah
up	en haut
	ohn oa
inside	à l'intérieur
	ah lahntayryuhr
outside	à l'extérieur
	ah lehxtayryuhr
behind	derrière
	dehryehr
at the front	à l'avant
	ah lahvohn
at the back	à l'arrière
	ah lahryehr
in the north	au nord
	oa nor
to the south	vers le sud
	vehr luh sewd
from the west	venant de l'ouest
	vuhnohn duh lwehst
from the east	venant de l'est
	vuhnohn duh lehst

1.7 What does that sign say?

See also **5.4 Traffic signs**

à louer
for hire
à vendre
for sale
accueil
reception
animaux interdits
no pets allowed
ascenseur
lift
attention à la marche
mind the step
attention chien méchant
beware of the dog
caisse
pay here
complet
full
dames
ladies
danger
danger
défense de toucher
please do not touch
eau non potable
no drinking water
en panne
out of order
entrée

entrance
entrée gratuite
admission free
entrée interdite
no entry
escalier roulant
escalator
escalier
stairs
escalier de secours
fire escape
...étage
...floor
frein de secours
emergency brake
haute tension
high voltage
heures d'ouverture
opening hours
interdit d'allumer un feu
no open fires
interdit de fumer
no smoking
interdit de photographier
no photographs
liquidation de stock
closing-down sale
messieurs
gents/gentlemen

ne pas déranger s'il vous plaît
do not disturb please
ouvert/fermé
open/closed
peinture fraîche
wet paint
pelouse interdite
keep off the grass
premiers soins
first aid
propriété privée
private (property)
renseignements
information
réservé
reserved
risque d'incendie
fire hazard
soldes
sale
sortie
exit
sortie de secours
emergency exit
pousser/tirer
push/pull
toilettes, wc
toilets

a	*ah*	comme Anatole	*kom ahnnahtol*
b	*bay*	comme Berthe	*kom behrt*
c	*say*	comme Célestin	*kom saylehstahn*
d	*day*	comme Désiré	*kom dayzeeray*
e	*uh*	comme Eugène	*kom uhjhehn*
f	*ehf*	comme François	*kom frohnswah*
g	*jhay*	comme Gaston	*kom gahstawn*
h	*ash*	comme Henri	*kom ohnree*
i	*ee*	comme Irma	*kom eermah*
j	*jhee*	comme Joseph	*kom jhosehf*
k	*kah*	comme Kléber	*kom klaybehr*
l	*ehl*	comme Louis	*kom looee*
m	*ehm*	comme Marcel	*kom mahrsehl*
n	*ehn*	comme Nicolas	*kom neekolah*
o	*oh*	comme Oscar	*kom oskahr*
p	*pay*	comme Pierre	*kom pyehr*
q	*kew*	comme Quintal	*kom kahntal*
r	*ehr*	comme Raoul	*kom rahool*
s	*ehs*	comme Suzanne	*kom sewzahnn*
t	*tay*	comme Thérèse	*kom tayrehz*
u	*ew*	comme Ursule	*kom ewrsewl*
v	*vee*	comme Victor	*kom veektor*
w	*doobluhvay*	comme William	*kom weelyahm*
x	*eex*	comme Xavier	*kom gsahvyay*
y	*eegrehk*	comme Yvonne	*kom eevon*
z	*zehd*	comme Zoé	*kom zoa-ay*

1.9 Personal details

last/family name	nom *nawn*
first name(s)	prénom(s) *praynawn*
initials	initiales *eeneesyahl*
address (street/number)	adresse (rue/numéro) *ahdrehs (rew/newmayroa)*
post code/town	code postal/ville *kod postahl/veel*
sex (male/female)	sexe (m/f) *sehx (ehm/ehf)*
nationality	nationalité *nahsyonahleetay*
date of birth	date de naissance *daht duh nehsohns*
place of birth	lieu de naissance *lyuh duh nehsohns*
occupation	profession *profehsyawn*
married/single/divorced	marié(e) /célibataire/divorcé(e) *mahreeay/sayleebahtehr/deevorsay*
widowed	veuf/veuve *vuhf/vuhv*
(number of) children	(nombre d')enfants *(nawnbr d)ohnfohn*

identity card/passport/
  driving licence number
	numéro de carte d'identité/ passeport/
	  permis de conduire
	*newmayroa duh kahrt deedohnteetay/
	  pahspor/pehrmee duh kawndweer*

place and date of issue	lieu et date de délivrance *lyuh ay daht duh dayleevrohns*

2. Courtesies

● It is usual in France to shake hands on meeting and parting company. Female friends and relatives may kiss each other on both cheeks when meeting and parting company. With men this varies according to the region. It is also polite to say monsieur and madame quite systematically as part of a greeting, e.g. *Bonjour, monsieur; au revoir, madame.*

● The English 'you' is expressed in French by either '*tu*' or '*vous*'. '*Tu*' is the more familiar form of address, used to talk to someone close or used between young people or when adults are talking to young children. '*Vous*' is the more formal and polite form of address. '*On*' is the generalised form of '*nous*' meaning people in general ('one' and 'we' in English).

2.1 Greetings

Hello, Mr Smith.	Bonjour monsieur Smith.
	bawnjhoor muhsyuh dewpawn
Hello, Mrs Jones.	Bonjour madame Jones.
	bawnjhoor mahdahm dewrohn
Hello, Peter.	Salut, Pierre.
	sahlew, pyehr
Hi, Helen.	Ça va, Hélène?
	sah vah, aylehn?
Good morning, madam.	Bonjour madame.
	bawnjhoor mahdahm
Good afternoon, sir.	Bonjour monsieur.
	bawnjhoor muhsyuh
Good evening.	Bonsoir.
	bawhnswahr
How are you?	Comment allez-vous?
	komohn tahlay voo?
Fine, thank you, and you?	Très bien et vous?
	treh byahn ay voo?
Very well.	Très bien.
	treh byahn

Not very well.	Pas très bien.
	pah treh byahn
Not too bad.	Ça va.
	sah vah
I'd better be going.	Je m'en vais.
	jhuh mohn veh
I have to be going.	Je dois partir.
	jhuh dwah pahrteer
Someone's waiting for me.	On m'attend.
	awn mahtohn
Bye!	Salut!
	sahlew!
Goodbye.	Au revoir.
	oa ruhvwahr
See you soon.	A bientôt.
	ah byahntoa
See you later.	A tout à l'heure.
	ah too tah luhr
See you in a little while.	A tout de suite.
	ah toot sweet
Sleep well.	Dormez bien/dors bien.
	dormay byahn, dor byahn
Good night.	Bonne nuit.
	bon nwee
Have fun.	Amuse-toi bien.
	ahmewz twah byahn
Good luck.	Bonne chance.
	bon shahns
Have a nice holiday.	Bonnes vacances.
	bon vahkohns
Have a good trip.	Bon voyage.
	bawn vwahyahjh
Thank you, you too.	Merci, de même.
	mehrsee, duh mehm
Say hello to...for me.	Mes amitiés à...
	may zahmeetyay ah...

2.2 How to ask a question

Who?	Qui? *kee?*
Who's that?	Qui est-ce? *kee ehs?*
What?	Quoi? *kwah?*
What's there to see here?	Qu'est-ce qu'on peut voir ici? *kehsk awn puh vwahr eesee?*
What kind of hotel is that?	C'est quelle sorte d'hôtel? *seh kehl sort doatehl?*
Where?	Où? *oo?*
Where's the toilet?	Où sont les toilettes? *oo sawn lay twahleht?*
Where are you going?	Où allez-vous? *oo ahlay voo?*
Where are you from?	D'où venez-vous? *doo vuhnay voo?*
How?	Comment? *komohn?*
How far is that?	C'est loin? *seh lwahn?*
How long does that take?	Combien de temps faut-il? *kawnbyahn duh tohn foa teel?*
How long is the trip?	Combien de temps dure le voyage? *kawnbyahn duh tohn dewr luh vwahyahjh?*
How much?	Combien? *kawnbyahn?*
How much is this?	C'est combien? *seh kawnbyahn?*
What time is it?	Quelle heure est-il? *kehl uhr eh teel?*
Which?	Quel? Quels?/Quelle? Quelles? *kehl?*

Which glass is mine?	Quel est mon verre?	*kehl eh mawn vehr?*
When?	Quand?	*kohn?*
When are you leaving?	Quand partez-vous?	*kohn pahrtay voo?*
Why?	Pourquoi?	*poorkwah?*
Could you...me?	Pouvez-vous me...?	*poovay voo muh...?*
Could you help me, please?	Pouvez-vous m'aider s'il vous plaît?	*poovay voo mayday seel voo pleh?*
Could you point that out to me?	Pouvez-vous me l'indiquer?	*poovay voo muh lahndeekay?*
Could you come with me, please?	Pouvez-vous m'accompagner s'il vous plaît?	*poovay voo mahkawnpahnnyay seel voo pleh?*
Could you...	Voulez-vous...?	*voolay voo...?*
Could you reserve some tickets for me, please?	Voulez-vous me réserver des places s'il vous plaît?	*voolay voo muh rayzehrvay day plahs seel voo pleh?*
Do you know...?	Connaissez-vous...?	*konehssay voo...?*
Do you know another hotel, please?	Vous connaissez peut-être un autre hôtel?	*voo konehssay puh tehtr uhn noatr oatehl?*
Do you know whether...?	Savez-vous si...?	*sahvay voo see...?*
Do you have a...?	Avez-vous un...?	*ahvay voo zuhn...?*

Do you have a vegetarian dish, please?	Vous avez peut-être un plat sans viande?
	voo zahvay puh tehtr uhn plah sohn vyohnd?
I'd like...	Je voudrais...
	jhuh voodreh...
I'd like a kilo of apples, please.	Je voudrais un kilo de pommes.
	jhuh voodreh zuhn keeloa duh pom
Can I...?	Puis-je...?
	pwee jhuh...?
Can I take this?	Puis-je prendre ceci?
	pwee jhuh prohndr suhsee?
Can I smoke here?	Puis-je fumer ici?
	pwee jhuh fewmay eesee?
Could I ask you something?	Puis-je vous demander quelque chose?
	pwee jhuh voo duhmohnday kehlkuh shoaz?

2.3 How to reply

Yes, of course.	Oui, bien sûr.
	wee, byahn sewr
No, I'm sorry.	Non, je suis désolé.
	nawn, jhuh swee dayzolay
Yes, what can I do for you?	Oui, que puis-je faire pour vous?
	wee, kuh pwee jhuh fehr poor voo?
Just a moment, please.	Un moment s'il vous plaît.
	uhn momohn seel voo pleh
No, I don't have time now.	Non, je n'ai pas le temps en ce moment.
	nawn, jhuh nay pah luh tohn ohn suh momohn
No, that's impossible.	Non, c'est impossible.
	nawn, seh tahnposseebl
I think so.	Je le crois bien.
	jhuh luh krwah byahn

I agree.	Je le pense aussi.
	jhuh luh pohns oasee
I hope so too.	Je l'espère aussi.
	jhuh lehspehr oasee
No, not at all.	Non, absolument pas.
	nawn, ahbsolewmohn pah
No, no-one.	Non, personne.
	nawn, pehrson
No, nothing.	Non, rien.
	nawn, ryahn
That's (not) right.	C'est (ce n'est pas) exact.
	seht (suh neh pahz) ehgzah
I (don't) agree.	Je suis (je ne suis pas) d'accord avec vous.
	jhuh swee (jhuh nuh swee pah) dahkor ahvehk voo
All right.	C'est bien.
	seh byahn
Okay.	D'accord.
	dahkor
Perhaps.	Peut-être.
	puh tehtr
I don't know.	Je ne sais pas.
	jhuh nuh seh pah

2.4 Thank you

Thank you.	Merci/merci bien.
	mehrsee/mehrsee byahn
You're welcome.	De rien/avec plaisir.
	duh ryahn/ahvehk playzeer
Thank you very much.	Merci beaucoup.
	mehrsee boakoo
It's very kind of you.	C'est aimable de votre part.
	seh taymahbl duh votr pahr

I enjoyed it very much.	C'était un réel plaisir.
	sayteh tuhn rayehl playzeer
Thank you for your trouble.	Je vous remercie pour la peine.
	jhuh voo ruhmehrsee poor lah pehn
You shouldn't have.	Vous n'auriez pas dû.
	voo noaryay pah dew
That's all right.	Pas de problème.
	pah duh problehm

2.5 Sorry

Excuse me.	Excusez-moi.
	ehxkewzay mwah
Sorry!	Pardon!
	pahrdawn!
I'm sorry, I didn't know...	Pardon, je ne savais pas que...
	pahrdawn jhuh nuh sahveh pah kuh...
I do apologise.	Excusez-moi.
	ehxkewzay mwah
I'm sorry.	Je suis désolé.
	jhuh swee dayzolay
I didn't do it on purpose, it was an accident.	Je ne l'ai pas fait. exprès, c'était un accident.
	jhuh ne lay pah feh ehxpreh, sayteh tuhn nahxeedohn
That's all right.	Ce n'est pas grave.
	suh neh pah grahv
Never mind.	Ça ne fait rien.
	sah nuh feh ryahn
It could've happened to anyone.	Ça peut arriver à tout le monde.
	sah puh ahreevay ah too luh mawnd

Which do you prefer?
Qu'est-ce que vous préférez?
kehs kuh voo prayfayray?

What do you think?
Qu'en penses-tu?
kohn pohns tew?

Don't you like dancing?
Tu n'aimes pas danser?
tew nehm pah dohnsay?

I don't mind.
Ça m'est égal.
sah meh taygahl

Well done!
Très bien!
treh byahn!

Not bad!
Pas mal!
pah mahl!

Great!
Génial!
jhaynyahl!

Wonderful!
Super!
sewpehr!

It's really nice here!
C'est drôlement agréable ici!
seh droalmohn ahgrayahbl eesee!

How nice!
Pas mal, chouette!
pah mahl, shweht!

How nice for you!
C'est formidable!
seh formeedahbl!

I'm (not) very happy with...
Je suis (ne suis pas) très satisfait(e) de...
jhuh swee (nuh swee pah) treh sahteesfeh(t) duh...

I'm glad...
Je suis content(e) que...
jhuh swee kawntohn(t) kuh...

I'm having a great time.
Je m'amuse beaucoup.
jhuh mahmewz boakoo

I'm looking forward to it.
Je m'en réjouis.
jhuh mohn rayjhwee

I hope it'll work out.
J'espère que cela réussira.
jhehspehr kuh suhlah rayewseerah

That's ridiculous!
C'est nul!
seh newl!

37

That's terrible!	Quelle horreur!
	kehl oruhr!
What a pity!	C'est dommage!
	seh domahjh!
That's filthy!	C'est dégoûtant!
	seh daygootohn!
What a load of rubbish!	C'est ridicule/C'est absurde!
	seh reedeekewl/seh tahbsewrd!
I don't like...	Je n'aime pas...
	jhuh nehm pah...
I'm bored to death.	Je m'ennuie à mourir.
	jhuh mohnnwee ah mooreer
I've had enough.	J'en ai assez/ras le bol.
	jhohn nay ahsay/rahl bol
This is no good.	Ce n'est pas possible.
	suh neh pah posseebl
I was expecting something completely different.	Je m'attendais à quelque chose de très différent.
	jhuh mahtohndeh ah kehlkuh shoaz duh treh deefayrohn

3. Conversation

I don't speak any/ I speak a little...	Je ne parle pas/je parle un peu... *jhuh nuh pahrl pah/jhuh pahrl uhn puh..*
I'm English.	Je suis anglais/anglaise. *jhuh swee zohngleh/zohnglehz*
I'm Scottish.	Je suis écossais/écossaise. *jhuh swee zaykosseh/zaykossehz*
I'm Irish.	Je suis irlandais/irlandaise. *jhuh swee zeerlohndeh/zeerlohndehz*
I'm Welsh.	Je suis gallois/galloise. *jhuh swee gahlwah/gahlwahz*
Do you speak English/French/ German?	Parlez-vous anglais/français/allemand? *pahrlay voo ohngleh/ frohnseh/ahlmohn?*
Is there anyone who speaks...?	Y a-t-il quelqu'un qui parle...? *ee yah teel kehlkuhn kee pahrl...?*
I beg your pardon?	Que dites-vous? *kuh deet voo?*
I (don't) understand.	Je (ne) comprends (pas). *jhuh (nuh) kawnprohn (pah)*
Do you understand me?	Me comprenez-vous? *me kawnpruhnay voo?*
Could you repeat that, please?	Voulez-vous répéter s'il vous plaît? *voolay voo raypaytay seel voo pleh?*
Could you speak more slowly, please?	Pouvez-vous parler plus lentement? *poovay voo pahrlay plew lohntmohn?*
What does that word mean?	Qu'est-ce que ce mot veut dire? *kehs kuh suh moa vuh deer?*
Is that similar to/the same as...?	Est-ce (environ) la même chose que...? *ehs (ohnveerawn) lah mehm shoaz kuh...?*
Could you write that down for me, please?	Pouvez-vous me l'écrire? *poovay voo muh laykreer?*
Could you spell that for me, please?	Pouvez-vous me l'épeler? *poovay voo muh laypuhlay?*

Could you point that out in this phrase book, please?
Pouvez-vous me le montrer dans ce guide de conversation?
poovay voo muh luh mawntray dohn suh gueed duh kawnvehrsahsyawn?

One moment, please, I have to look it up.
Un moment, je dois le chercher.
uhn momohn, jhuh dwah luh shehrshay

I can't find the word/ the sentence.
Je ne trouve pas le mot/la phrase.
jhuh nuh troov pah luh moa/lah frahz

How do you say that in...?
Comment dites-vous cela en...?
komohn deet voo suhlah ohn...?

How do you pronounce that?
Comment prononcez-vous cela?
komohn pronawnsay voo suhlah?

3.2 Introductions

My name's...
Je m'appelle...
jhuh mahpehl...

I'm...
Je suis...
jhuh swee...

What's your name?
Comment vous appelez-vous?
komohn voo zahpuhlay voo?

May I introduce...?
Puis-je vous présenter?
pwee jhuh voo prayzohntay?

This is my wife/daughter/ mother/girlfriend.
Voici ma femme/fille/mère/mon amie.
vwahsee mah fahm/feey/mehr/mawn nahmee

- my husband/son/father/ boyfriend.
Voici mon mari/fils/père/ami.
vwahsee mawn mahree/fees/pehr/ ahmee

How do you do?
Enchanté(e).
ohnshohntay

Pleased to meet you.	Je suis heureux(se) de faire votre connaissance.
	jhuh swee zuhruh(z) duh fehr votr kohnehssohns
Where are you from?	D'où venez-vous?
	doo vuhnay voo?
I'm from England/Scotland/ Ireland/Wales.	Je viens d'Angleterre/d'Ecosse/ d'Irlande/du pays de Galles.
	jhuh vyahn dohngluhtehr/daykos/ deerlohnd/dew payee duh gahl
What city do you live in?	Vous habitez dans quelle ville?
	voo zahbeetay dohn kehl veel?
In..., It's near...	A...C'est à côté de...
	ah...seh tah koatay duh...
Have you been here long?	Etes-vous ici depuis longtemps?
	eht voo zeesee duhpwee lawntohn?
A few days.	Depuis quelques jours.
	depwee kehlkuh jhoor
How long are you staying here?	Combien de temps restez-vous ici?
	kawnbyahn duh tohn rehstay voo zeesee?
We're (probably) leaving tomorrow/in two weeks.	Nous partirons (probablement) demain/ dans quinze jours.
	noo pahrteerawn (probahbluhmohn) duhmahn/dohn kahnz jhoor
Where are you staying?	Où logez-vous?
	oo lojhay voo?
In a hotel/an apartment.	Dans un hôtel/appartement.
	dohn zuhn noatehl/ahpahrtuhmohn
On a camp site.	Dans un camping.
	dohn zuhn kohnpeeng
With friends/relatives.	Chez des amis/chez de la famille.
	shay day zahmee/shay duh lah fahmeey
Are you here on your own/ with your family?	Etes-vous ici seul/avec votre famille?
	eht voo zeesee suhl/ahvehk votr fahmeey?
I'm on my own.	Je suis seul(e).
	jhuh swee suhl

I'm with my partner/wife/ husband.
Je suis avec mon ami(e)/ma femme/ mon mari.
jhuh swee zahvehk mawn nahmee/mah fahm/mawn mahree

- with my family.
Je suis avec ma famille.
jhuh swee zahvehk mah fahmeey

- with relatives.
Je suis avec de la famille.
jhuh swee zahvehk duh lah fahmeey

- with a friend/friends.
Je suis avec un ami/une amie /des amis.
jhuh swee zahvehk uhn nahmee/ewn ahmee/day zahmee

Are you married?
Etes-vous marié(e)?
eht voo mahreeay?

Do you have a boyfriend/girlfriend?
As-tu un petit ami (une petite amie)?
ah tew uhn puhtee tahmee (ewn puhteet ahmee)?

That's none of your business.
Cela ne vous regarde pas.
suhlah nuh voo ruhgahrd pah

I'm married.
Je suis marié(e).
jhuh swee mahreeay

- single.
Je suis célibataire.
jhuh swee sayleebahtehr

- separated.
Je suis séparé(e).
jhuh swee saypahray

- divorced.
Je suis divorcé(e).
jhuh swee deevorsay

- a widow/widower.
Je suis veuf/veuve.
jhuh swee vuhf/vuhv

I live alone/with someone.
J'habite tout(e) seul(e)/avec quelqu'un.
jhahbeet too suhl(toot suhl)/ahvehk kehlkuhn

Do you have any children/ grandchildren?
Avez-vous des enfants/petits-enfants?
ahvay voo day zohnfohn/puhtee zohnfohn?

How old are you?
Quel âge avez-vous?
kehl ahjh ahvay voo?

How old is he/she?	Quel âge a-t-il/a-t-elle?
	kehl ahjh ah teel/ah tehl?
I'm...years old.	J'ai...ans.
	jhay...ohn
He's/she's...years old.	Il/elle a...ans.
	eel/ehl ah...ohn
What do you do for a living?	Quel est votre métier?
	kehl eh votr maytyay?
I work in an office.	Je travaille dans un bureau.
	jhuh trahvahy dohn zuhn bewroa
I'm a student/I'm at school.	Je fais des études/je vais à l'école.
	jhuh feh day zaytewd/jhuh veh zah laykol
I'm unemployed.	Je suis au chômage.
	jhuh swee zoa shoamajh
I'm retired.	Je suis retraité(e).
	jhuh swee ruhtrehtay
Do you like your job?	Votre travail vous plaît?
	votr trahvahy voo pleh?
Most of the time.	Ça dépend.
	sah daypohn
I prefer holidays.	J'aime mieux les vacances.
	Jhehm myuh lay vahkohns

3.3 Starting/ending a conversation

Could I ask you something?	Puis-je vous poser une question?
	pwee jhuh voo poazay ewn kehstyawn?
Excuse me.	Excusez-moi.
	ehxkewsay mwah
Excuse me, could you help me?	Pardon, pouvez-vous m'aider?
	pahrdawn, poovay voo mayday?
Yes, what's the problem?	Oui, qu'est-ce qui se passe?
	wee, kehs kee suh pahss?
What can I do for you?	Que puis-je faire pour vous?
	kuh pwee jhuh fehr poor voo?

Sorry, I don't have time now.	Excusez-moi, je n'ai pas le temps maintenant.
	ehxkewzay mwah, jhuh nay pah luh tohn mahntuhnohn
Do you have a light?	Vous avez du feu?
	voo zahvay dew fuh?
May I join you?	Puis-je m'asseoir à côté de vous?
	pwee jhuh mahsswahr ah koatay duh voo?
Could you take a picture of me/us? Press this button.	Voulez-vous me/nous prendre en photo? Appuyez sur ce bouton.
	voolay voo muh/noo prohndr ohn foatoa? ahpweeyay sewr suh bootawn
Leave me alone.	Laissez-moi tranquille.
	laysay mwah trohnkeey
Get lost!	Fichez le camp!
	feeshay luh kohn!

3.4 Congratulations and condolences

Happy birthday/ many happy returns.	Bon anniversaire/bonne fête.
	bohn nahnneevehrsehr/bon feht
Please accept my condolences.	Mes condoléances.
	may kawndolayohns
I'm very sorry for you.	Cela me peine beaucoup pour vous.
	suhlah muh pehn boakoo poor voo

3.5 A chat about the weather

See also **1.5 The weather**

It's so hot/cold today!	Qu'est-ce qu'il fait chaud/froid aujourd'hui!
	kehs keel feh shoa/frwah oajhoordwee!
Nice weather, isn't it?	Il fait beau, n'est-ce pas?
	eel feh boa, nehs pah?
What a wind/storm!	Quel vent/orage!
	kehl vohn/orahjh!
All that rain/snow!	Quelle pluie/neige!
	kehl plwee/nehjh!
All that fog!	Quel brouillard!
	kehl brooy-yahr!
Has the weather been like this for long here?	Fait-il ce temps-là depuis longtemps?
	feh teel suh tohn lah duhpwee lawntohn?
Is it always this hot/cold here?	Fait-il toujours aussi chaud/froid ici?
	feh teel toojhoor oasee shoa/frwah eesee?
Is it always this dry/wet here?	Fait-il toujours aussi sec/humide ici?
	feh teel toojhoor oasee sehk/ewmeed eesee?
What will the weather be like tomorrow?	Quel temps fera-t-il demain?
	kehl tohn fuhra teel duhmahn?

3.6 Hobbies

Do you have any hobbies?	Avez-vous des passe-temps?
	ahvay voo day pahs tohn?
I like painting/reading/ photography/DIY	J'aime peindre/lire/la photo/le bricolage
	jhehm pahndr/leer/lah foatoa/luh breekolahjh
I like music.	J'aime la musique.
	jhehm lah mewzeek

I like playing the guitar/piano.	J'aime jouer de la guitare/du piano.
	jhehm jhooay duh lah gueetahr/dew pyahnoa
I like going to the movies.	J'aime aller au cinéma.
	jhehm ahlay oa seenaymah
I like travelling/sport/ fishing/walking.	J'aime voyager/faire du sport/ la pêche/me promener.
	jhehm vwahyahjhay/fehr dew spor/lah pehsh/muh promuhnay

3.7 Being the host(ess)

See also **4 Eating out**

Can I offer you a drink?	Puis-je vous offrir quelque chose à boire?
	pwee jhuh voo zofreer kehlkuh shoaz ah bwahr?
What would you like to drink?	Que désires-tu boire?
	kuh dayzeer tew bwahr?
Something non-alcoholic, please.	De préférence quelque chose sans alcool.
	duh prayfayrohns kehlkuh shoaz sohn zahlkol
Would you like a cigarette/ cigar/to roll your own?	Voulez-vous une cigarette/un cigare/ rouler une cigarette?
	voolay voo zewn seegahreht/uhn seegahr/roolay ewn seegahreht?
I don't smoke.	Je ne fume pas.
	jhuh nuh fewm pah

3.8 Invitations

Are you doing anything tonight?
Faites-vous quelque chose ce soir?
feht voo kehlkuh shoaz suh swahr?

Do you have any plans for today/this afternoon/tonight?
Avez-vous déjà fait des projets pour aujourd'hui/cet après-midi/ce soir?
ahvay voo dayjhah feh day projheh poor oa-jhoordwee/seht ahpreh meedee/suh swahr?

Would you like to go out with me?
Aimeriez-vous sortir avec moi?
aymuhryay voo sorteer ahvehk mwah?

Would you like to go dancing with me?
Aimeriez-vous aller danser avec moi?
aymuhryay voo zahlay dohnsay ahvehk mwah?

Would you like to have lunch/dinner with me?
Aimeriez-vous déjeuner/dîner avec moi?
aymuhryay voo dayjhuhnay/deenay ahvehk mwah?

Would you like to come to the beach with me?
Aimeriez-vous aller à la plage avec moi?
aymuhryay voo zahlay ah lah plahjh ahvehk mwah?

Would you like to come into town with us?
Aimeriez-vous aller en ville avec nous?
aymuhryay voo zahlay ohn veel ahvehk noo?

Would you like to come and see some friends with us?
Aimeriez-vous aller chez des amis avec nous?
aymuhryay voo zahlay shay day zahmee ahvehk noo?

Shall we dance?
On danse?
awn dohns?

– sit at the bar?
On va s'asseoir au bar?
awn vah saswahr oa bahr?

– get something to drink?
On va boire quelque chose?
awn vah bwahr kehlkuh shoaz?

– go for a walk/drive?	On va marcher un peu/on va faire un tour en voiture?	*awn vah mahrshay uhn puh/awn vah fehr uhn toor ohn vwahtewr?*
Yes, all right.	Oui, d'accord.	*wee, dahkor*
Good idea.	Bonne idée.	*bon eeday*
No (thank you).	Non (merci).	*nawn (mehrsee)*
Maybe later.	Peut-être tout à l'heure.	*puh tehtr too tah luhr*
I don't feel like it.	Je n'en ai pas envie.	*jhuh nohn nay pah zohnvee*
I don't have time.	Je n'ai pas le temps.	*jhuh nay pah luh tohn*
I already have a date.	J'ai déjà un autre rendez-vous.	*jhay dayjhah uhn noatr rohnday voo*
I'm not very good at dancing/volleyball/swimming.	Je ne sais pas danser/jouer au volley/nager.	*jhuh nuh seh pah dohnsay/jhooay oa volay/nahjhay*

3.9 Paying a compliment

You look wonderful!	Vous avez l'air en pleine forme!
	voo zahvay lehr ohn plehn form!
I like your car!	Quelle belle voiture!
	kehl behl vwahtewr!
I like your ski outfit!	Quelle belle combinaison de ski!
	kehl behl kawnbeenehzawn duh skee!
You're a nice boy/girl.	Tu es un garçon/une fille sympathique.
	tew eh zuhn gahrsohn/ewn feey sahnpahteek
What a sweet child!	Quel adorable enfant!
	kehl ahdorahbl ohnfohn!
You're a wonderful dancer!	Vous dansez très bien!
	voo dohnsay treh byahn!
You're a wonderful cook!	Vous faites très bien la cuisine!
	voo feht treh byahn lah kweezeen!
You're a terrific football player!	Vous jouez très bien au football!
	voo jhooay treh byahn oa footbol!

3.10 Romance and relationships

I like being with you.	J'aime bien être près de toi.
	jhehm byahn ehtr preh duh twah
I've missed you so much.	Tu m'as beaucoup manqué.
	tew mah boakoo mohnkay
I dreamed about you.	J'ai rêvé de toi.
	jhay rehvay duh twah
I think about you all day.	Je pense à toi toute la journée.
	jhuh pohns ah twah toot lah jhoornay
You have such a sweet smile.	Tu souris si gentiment.
	tew sooree see jhohnteemohn
You have such beautiful eyes.	Tu as de si jolis yeux.
	tew ah duh see jhoalee zyuh
I'm in love with you.	Je suis amoureux/se de toi.
	jhuh swee zahmooruh(z) duh twah

'm in love with you too.	Moi aussi de toi.
	mwah oasee duh twah
love you.	Je t'aime.
	jhuh tehm
love you too.	Je t'aime aussi.
	jhuh tehm oasee
don't feel as strongly about you.	Je n'ai pas d'aussi forts sentiments pour toi.
	jhuh nay pah doasee for sohnteemohn poor twah
already have a boyfriend/girlfriend.	J'ai déjà un ami/une amie.
	jhay dayjhah uhn nahmee/ewn ahmee
'm not ready for that.	Je n'en suis pas encore là.
	jhuh nohn swee pah zohnkor lah
This is going too fast for me.	Ça va un peu trop vite.
	sah vah uhn puh troa veet
Take your hands off me.	Ne me touche pas.
	nuh muh toosh pah
Okay, no problem.	D'accord, pas de problème.
	dahkor, pah duh problehm
Will you stay with me tonight?	Tu restes avec moi cette nuit?
	tew rehst ahvehk mwah seht nwee?
'd like to go to bed with you.	J'aimerais coucher avec toi.
	jhehmuhreh kooshay ahvehk twah
Only if we use a condom.	Seulement en utilisant un préservatif.
	suhlmohn ohn newteeleezohn uhn prayzehrvahteef
We have to be careful about STDs.	Il faut être prudent à cause des MST.
	eel foa tehtr prewdohn ah koaz day ehm ehs tay
That's what they all say.	Ils disent tous pareil.
	eel deez toos pahrehy
We shouldn't take any risks.	Ne prenons aucun risque.
	nuh pruhnawn zoakuhn reesk
Do you have a condom?	Tu as un préservatif?
	tew ah zuhn prayzehrvahteef?

| No? In that case we won't do it. | Non? Alors je ne veux pas. |
| | *nawn? ahlor jhuh nuh vuh pah* |

3.11 Arrangements

When will I see you again?	Quand est-ce que je te revois?
	kohn tehs kuh jhuh tuh ruhvwah?
Are you free over the weekend?	Vous êtes/tu es libre ce week-end?
	voozeht/tew eh leebr suh week-ehnd?
What shall we arrange?	Que décidons-nous?
	kuh dayseedawn noo?
Where shall we meet?	Où nous retrouvons-nous?
	oo noo ruhtroovawn noo?
Will you pick me/us up?	Vous venez me/nous chercher?
	voo vuhnay muh/noo shehrshay?
Shall I pick you up?	Je viens vous/te chercher?
	jhuh vyahn voo/tuh shehrshay?
I have to be home by...	Je dois être à la maison à...heures.
	jhuh dwah zehtr ah lah mehzawn ah...uhr

3.12 Saying goodbye

I don't want to see you any more.	Je ne veux plus vous revoir.
	jhuh nuh vuh plew voo ruhvwahr
Can I take you home?	Puis-je vous raccompagner à la maison?
	pwee jhuh voo rahkawnpahnyay ah lah mehzawn?
Can I write/call you?	Puis-je vous écrire/téléphoner?
	pwee jhuh voo zaykreer/taylayfonay?
Will you write/call me?	M'écrirez-vous/me téléphonerez-vous?
	maykreeray voo/muh taylayfonuhray voo?

Can I have your address/ phone number?

Puis-je avoir votre adresse/numéro de téléphone?

pwee jhahvwahr votr ahdrehs/ newmayroa duh taylayfon?

Thanks for everything.

Merci pour tout.

mehrsee poor too

It was very nice.

C'était très agréable.

sayteh treh zahgrayahbl

Say hello to...

Présentez mes amitiés à...

prayzohntay may zahmeetyay ah...

Good luck.

Bonne chance.

bon shohns

When will you be back?

Quand est-ce que tu reviens?

kohn tehs kuh tew ruhvyahn?

I'll be waiting for you.

Je t'attendrai.

jhuh tahtohndray

I'd like to see you again.

J'aimerais te revoir.

jhehmuhreh tuh ruhvwahr

I hope we meet again soon.

J'espère que nous nous reverrons bientôt.

jhehspehr kuh noo noo ruhvehrawn byahntoa

You are welcome.

Vous êtes le/la bienvenu(e).

voozeht luh/lah byahnvuhnew

4. Eating out

● In France people usually have three meals:

1 *Le petit déjeuner* (breakfast) approx. between 7.30 and 10am.
Breakfast is light and consists of *café au lait* (white coffee) or lemon tea,
a croissant, or slices of *baguette* (French bread), with butter and jam.

2 *Le déjeuner* (lunch) approx. between midday and 2pm. Lunch
always includes a hot dish and is the most important meal of the
day. Offices and shops often close and lunch is taken at home,
in a restaurant or canteen (in some factories and schools). It usually
consists of four courses:

– starter
– main course
– cheese
– dessert

3 *Le dîner* (dinner) between 7.30 and 9pm. Dinner is a light hot meal,
usually taken with the family.

At around 5pm, a special snack (*le goûter*) is served to children, usually a
roll or slices of baguette and biscuits with some chocolate.

4.1 On arrival

I'd like to book a table for seven o'clock, please?	Puis-je réserver une table pour sept heures? *pwee jhuh rayzehrvay ewn tahbl poor seht uhr?*
I'd like a table for two, please.	Une table pour deux personnes s'il vous plaît. *ewn tahbl poor duh pehrson seel voo pleh*
We've/we haven't booked.	Nous (n')avons (pas) réservé. *noo zahvawn/noo nahvawn pah rayzehrvay*
Is the restaurant open yet?	Le restaurant est déjà ouvert? *luh rehstoarohn eh dayjhah oovehr?*
What time does the restaurant open/close?	A quelle heure ouvre/ferme le restaurant? *ah kehl uhr oovr/fehrm luh rehstoarohn?*

Vous avez réservé?	Do you have a reservation?
A quel nom?	What name, please?
Par ici, s'il vous plaît.	This way, please.
Cette table est réservée.	This table is reserved.
Nous aurons une table de libre dans un quart d'heure.	We'll have a table free in fifteen minutes.
Voulez-vous patienter (au bar)?	Would you like to wait (at the bar)?

Can we wait for a table?	Pouvons-nous attendre qu'une table soit libre?
	poovawn noo zahtohndr kewn tahbl swah leebr?
Do we have to wait long?	Devons-nous attendre longtemps?
	devawn noo zahtohndr lawntohn?
Is this seat taken?	Est-ce que cette place est libre?
	ehs kuh seht plahs eh leebr?
Could we sit here/there?	Pouvons-nous nous asseoir ici/là-bas?
	poovawn noo noo zahswahr eesee/lahbah?
Can we sit by the window?	Pouvons-nous nous asseoir près de la fenêtre?
	poovawn noo noo zahswahr preh duh lah fuhnehtr?
Can we eat outside?	Pouvons-nous aussi manger dehors?
	poovawn noo zoasee mohnjhay duh-ohr?
Do you have another chair for us?	Avez-vous encore une chaise?
	ahvay voo zohnkor ewn shehz?
Do you have a highchair?	Avez-vous une chaise haute?
	ahvay voo zewn shehz oat?

Could you warm up this bottle/jar for me?	Pouvez-vous me réchauffer ce biberon/ce petit pot?
	poovay voo muh rayshoafay suh beebuhrawn/suh puhtee poa?
Not too hot, please.	Pas trop chaud s'il vous plaît.
	pah troa shoa seel voo pleh
Is there somewhere I can change the baby's nappy?	Y a-t-il ici une pièce où je peux m'occuper du bébé?
	ee ya teel eesee ewn pyehs oo jhuh puh mokewpay dew baybay?
Where are the toilets?	Où sont les toilettes?
	oo sawn lay twahleht?

4.2 Ordering

Waiter!/Waitress!	Garçon!/S'il vous plaît!
	gahrsawn!/seel voo play!
Madam!	Madame!
	mahdahm!
Sir!	Monsieur!
	muhsyuh!
We'd like something to eat/a drink.	Nous aimerions manger/boire quelque chose.
	noo zaymuhryawn mohnjhay/bwahr kehlkuh shoaz
Could I have a quick meal?	Puis-je rapidement manger quelque chose?
	pwee jhuh rahpeedmohn mohnjhay kehlkuh shoaz?
We don't have much time.	Nous avons peu de temps.
	noo zavawn puh duh tohn
We'd like to have a drink first.	Nous voulons d'abord boire quelque chose.
	noo voolawn dahbor bwahr kehlkuh shoaz

Could we see the menu/wine list, please?	Pouvons-nous avoir la carte/la carte des vins?
	poovawn noo zahvwahr lah kahrt/lah kahrt day vahn?
Do you have a menu in English?	Vous avez un menu en anglais?
	voo zahvay zuhn muhnew ohn nohngleh?
Do you have a dish of the day?	Vous avez un plat du jour?
	voo zahvay zuhn plah dew jhoor?
We haven't made a choice yet.	Nous n'avons pas encore choisi.
	noo nahvawn pah zohnkor shwahzee
What do you recommend?	Qu'est-ce que vous nous conseillez?
	kehs kuh voo noo kawnsayay?
What are the specialities of the region/the house?	Quelles sont les spécialités de cette région/de la maison?
	kehl sawn lay spaysyahleetay duh seht rayjhyawn/duh lah mehzawn?
Is this food kosher/halal?	Est-ce casher/hallal?
	ehs cahshehr/ahlahl?
I like strawberries/olives.	J'aime les fraises/les olives.
	jhehm lay frehz/lay zoleev
I don't like meat/fish/...	Je n'aime pas la viande/le poisson/...
	jhuh nehm pah lah vyohnd/luh pwahssawn/...

Vous désirez prendre un apéritif?	Would you like a drink first?
Vous avez déjà fait votre choix?	Have you decided?
Que désirez-vous boire?	What would you like to drink?
Bon appétit!	Enjoy your meal!
Vous désirez votre viande saignante, à point ou bien cuite?	Would you like your steak rare, medium or well done?
Vous désirez un dessert/ du café?	Would you like a dessert/coffee?

Does this food contain nuts?	Est-ce que cet aliment contient des arachides/fruits à coque?
	ehs kuh seht ahleemohn kawnteeahn day ahrahsheed/frewee ah kok?
What's this?	Qu'est-ce que c'est?
	kehs kuh seh?
Does it have...in it?	Y a-t-il du/de la/des...dedans?
	ee ya teel dew/duh lah/day...duhdohn?
What does it taste like?	A quoi cela ressemble-t-il?
	ah kwah suhlah ruhsohnbluh teel?
Is this a hot or a cold dish?	Ce plat, est-il chaud ou froid?
	suh plah, eh teel shoa oo frwah?
Is this sweet?	Ce plat, est-il sucré?
	suh plah, eh teel sewkray?
Is this spicy?	Ce plat, est-il épicé?
	suh plah, eh teel aypeesay?
Do you have anything else, please?	Vous avez peut-être autre chose?
	voo zahvay puh tehtr oatr shoaz?
I'm on a salt-free diet.	Le sel m'est interdit.
	luh sehl meh tahntehrdee
I can't eat pork.	La viande de porc m'est interdite.
	lah vyohnd duh por meh tahntehrdeet
– sugar.	Le sucre m'est interdit.
	luh sewkr meh tahntehrdee
– fatty foods.	Le gras m'est interdit.
	luh grah meh tahntehrdee
– (hot) spices.	Les épices (fortes) me sont interdites.
	lay zaypees (fort) muh sawn tahntehrdeet
I have an allergy to nuts/seafood/wheat.	Je suis allergique aux arachides/fruits à coque/fruits de mer/au blé.
	juh sewee ahlehrjik oh ahrahsheed/frewee ah kok/frewee duh mehr/oh blay
I'll have what those people are having.	J'aimerais la même chose que ces personnes-là.
	jhehmuhreh lah mehm shoaz kuh say pehrson lah

I'd like…	J'aimerais…
	jhehmuhreh…
We're not having a starter.	Nous ne prenons pas d'entrée.
	noo nuh pruhnawn pah dohntray
The child will share what we're having.	L'enfant partagera notre menu.
	lohnfohn pahrtahjhuhrah notr muhnew
Could I have some more bread, please?	Encore du pain s'il vous plaît.
	ohnkor dew pahn seel voo pleh
– a bottle of water/wine.	Une autre bouteille d'eau/de vin.
	ewn oatr bootehy doa/duh vahn
– another helping of…	Une autre portion de…
	ewn oatr porsyawn duh…
– some salt and pepper.	Pouvez-vous apporter du sel et du poivre?
	poovay voo zahportay dew sehl ay dew pwahvr?
– a napkin.	Pouvez-vous apporter une serviette?
	poovay voo zahportay ewn sehrvyeht?
– a spoon.	Pouvez-vous apporter une cuillère?
	poovay voo zahportay ewn kweeyehr?
– an ashtray.	Pouvez-vous apporter un cendrier?
	poovay voo zahportay uhn sohndryay?
– some toothpicks.	Pouvez-vous apporter des cure-dents?
	poovay voo zahportay day kewr dohn?
– a glass of water.	Pouvez-vous apporter un verre d'eau?
	poovay voo zahportay uhn vehr doa?
– a straw (for the child).	Pouvez-vous apporter une paille (pour l'enfant)?
	poovay voo zahportay ewn paheey (poor lohnfohn)?
Enjoy your meal!	Bon appétit!
	bohn nahpaytee!
You too!	De même vous aussi.
	duh mehm voo zoasee
Cheers!	Santé!
	sohntay!

he next round's on me. La prochaine tournée est pour moi.
lah proshehn toornay eh poor mwah

ould we have a doggy bag, Pouvons-nous emporter les restes
  please?   pour notre chien?
*poovawn noo zohnportay lay rehst poor
  notr shyahn?*

4.3 The bill

ee also **8.2 Settling the bill**

low much is this dish? Quel est le prix de ce plat?
kehl eh luh pree duh suh plah?

ould I have the bill, please? L'addition s'il vous plaît.
lahdeesyawn seel voo pleh

ll together. Tout ensemble.
too tohnsohnbl

veryone pays separately. Chacun paye pour soi.
shahkuhn pehy poor swah

ould we have the menu Pouvons-nous revoir la carte?
  again, please? *poovawn noo ruhvwahr lah kahrt?*

he...is not on the bill. Le...n'est pas sur l'addition.
luh...neh pah sewr lahdeesyawn

4.4 Complaints

's taking a very long time. C'est bien long.
seh byahn lawn

Ve've been here an Nous sommes ici depuis une heure.
  hour already. *noo som zeesee duhpwee zewn uhr*

his must be a mistake. Cela doit être une erreur.
suhlah dwah tehtr ewn ehruhr

his is not what I ordered. Ce n'est pas ce que j'ai commandé.
suh neh pah suh kuh jhay komohnday

I ordered…	J'ai commandé un…
	jhay komohnday uhn…
There's a dish missing.	Il manque un plat.
	eel mohnk uhn plah
This is broken/not clean.	C'est cassé/ce n'est pas propre.
	seh kahssay/suh neh pah propr
The food's cold.	Le plat est froid.
	luh plah eh frwah
– not fresh.	Le plat n'est pas frais.
	luh plah neh pah freh
– too salty/sweet/spicy.	Le plat est trop salé/sucré/épicé.
	luh plah eh troa sahlay/sewkray/ aypeesay
The meat's not done.	La viande n'est pas cuite.
	lah vyohnd neh pah kweet
– overdone.	La viande est trop cuite.
	lah vyohnd eh troa kweet
– tough.	La viande est dure.
	lah vyohnd eh dewr
– off.	La viande est avariée.
	lah vyohnd eh tahvahryay
Could I have something else instead of this?	Vous pouvez me donner autre chose à la place?
	voo poovay muh donay oatr shoaz ah lah plahs?
The bill/this amount is not right.	L'addition/cette somme n'est pas exacte.
	lahdeesyawn/seht som neh pah zehgzahkt
We didn't have this.	Ceci nous ne l'avons pas eu.
	suhsee noo nuh lahvawn pah zew
There's no paper in the toilet.	Il n'y a plus de papier hygiénique dans les toilettes.
	eel nee yah plew duh pahpyay eejhyayneek dohn lay twahleht

| Will you call the manager, please? | Voulez-vous appeler le directeur s'il vous plaît? |
| | *voolay voo zahpuhlay luh deerehktuhr seel voo pleh?* |

4.5 Paying a compliment

That was a wonderful meal.	Nous avons très bien mangé.
	noo zahvawn treh byahn mohnjhay
The food was excellent.	Le repas était succulent.
	luh ruhpah ayteh sewkewlohn
The...in particular	Le...surtout était délicieux.
was delicious.	*luh...sewrtoo ayteh dayleesyuh*

4.6 The menu

apéritifs	gibier	plat principal
aperitifs	game	main course
boissons alcoolisées	hors d'oeuvres	potages
alcoholic beverages	starters	soups
boissons chaudes	légumes	service compris
hot beverages	vegetables	service included
carte des vins	plats chauds	spécialités
wine list	hot dishes	régionales
coquillages	plats froids	regional specialities
shellfish	cold dishes	viandes
desserts	plat du jour	meat dishes
sweets	dish of the day	volailles
fromages	pâtisserie	poultry
cheese	pastry	

agneau
lamb

ail
garlic

amandes
almonds

ananas
pineapple

anchois
anchovy

anguille
eel

anis
aniseed

apéritif
aperitif

artichaut
artichoke

asperge
asparagus

baguette
french stick

banane
banana

beurre
butter

biftec
steak

bière (bière pression)
beer (draught beer)

biscuit
biscuit

boeuf
beef

boissons alcoolisées
alcoholic beverages

boissons chaudes/ froides
hot/cold beverages

boudin noir/blanc
black/white pudding

brochet
pike

cabillaud
cod

café (noir/au lait)
coffee (black/white)

caille
quail

calmar
squid

canard
duck

câpres
capers

carpe
carp

carte des vins
wine list

céleri
celery

cerises
cherries

champignons
mushrooms

crème chantilly
cream (whipped)

châtaigne
chestnut

chausson aux pommes
apple turnover

chou-fleur
cauliflower

choucroute
sauerkraut

chou
cabbage

choux de Bruxelles
Brussels sprouts

citron
lemon

civet de lièvre
jugged hare

clou de girofle
clove

cocktails
cocktails

cognac
brandy

concombre
cucumber

confiture
jam

consommé
broth

coquillages
shellfish

coquilles
  Saint-Jacques
scallops

cornichon
gherkin

côte/côtelette
chop

côte de boeuf
T-bone steak

côte de porc
pork chop

côtelette d'agneau
lamb chop

côtelettes dans
  l'échine
spare rib

couvert
cutlery

crabe
crab

crêpes
pancakes

crevettes grises
shrimps

crevettes roses
prawns

croissant
croissant

croque monsieur
toasted ham and
  cheese sandwich

cru
raw

crustacés
seafood

cuisses de
  grenouilles
frog's legs

cuit (à l'eau)
boiled

dattes
dates

daurade
sea bream

dessert
sweet

eau minérale
  gazeuse/non
  gazeuse
sparkling/still
  mineral water

échalote
shallot

écrevisse
crayfish

endives
chicory

entrecôte
sirloin steak

entrées
first course

épices
spices

épinards
spinach

escargots
snails

farine
flour

fenouil
fennel

fèves
broad beans

figues
figs

filet de boeuf
fillet

filet mignon
fillet steak

filet de porc
tenderloin

fines herbes
herbs

foie gras
goose liver

fraises
strawberries

framboises
raspberries

frit	huîtres	loup de mer
fried	oysters	sea bass
friture	jambon blanc/	macaron
deep-fried	cru/fumé	macaroon
fromage	ham (cooked/Parma	maïs
cheese	style/smoked)	sweetcorn
fruit de la passion	jus de citron	épis de maïs
passion fruit	lemon juice	corn (on the cob)
fruits de la saison	jus de fruits	marron
seasonal fruits	fruit juice	chestnut
gaufres	jus d'orange	melon
waffles	orange juice	melon
gigot d'agneau	lait/demi-écrémé/	menu du jour/
leg of lamb	entier	à la carte
glace	milk/semi-skimmed/	menu of the day/
ice cream	full-cream	à la carte
glaçons	langouste	morilles
ice cubes	crayfish	morels
grillé	langoustine	moules
grilled	scampi	mussels
groseilles	langue	mousse au
redcurrants	tongue	chocolat
hareng	lapin	chocolate mousse
herring	rabbit	moutarde
haricots blancs	légumes	mustard
haricot beans	vegetables	myrtilles
haricots verts	lentilles	bilberries
french beans	lentils	noisette
homard	liqueur	hazelnut
lobster	liqueur	noix
hors d'oeuvre	lotte	walnut
starters	monkfish	

noix de veau
fillet of veal

oeuf à la coque/
  dur/au plat
egg soft/hard
  boiled/fried

oignon
onion

olives
olives

omelette
omelette

origan
oregano

pain au chocolat
chocolate bun

part
portion

pastis
pastis

pâtisserie
pastry

pêche
peach

petite friture
fried fish (whitebait
  or similar)

petits (biscuits)
  salés
savoury biscuits

petit pain
roll

petits pois
green peas

pigeon
pigeon

pintade
guinea fowl

plat du jour
dish of the day

plats froids/
  chauds
cold/hot courses

poire
pear

pois chiches
chick peas

poisson
fish

poivre
pepper

poivron
green/red pepper

pomme
apple

pommes de terre
potatoes

pommes frites
chips

poulet (blanc)
chicken (breast)

prune
plum

pruneaux
prunes

queue de boeuf
oxtail

ragoût
stew

ris de veau
sweetbread

riz
rice

rôti de boeuf (rosbif)
roast beef

rouget
red mullet

saignant
rare

salade verte
lettuce

salé/sucré
salted/sweet

sandwich
sandwich

saumon
salmon

sel
salt

service compris/
  non compris
service (not) included

sole
sole

soupe
soup

soupe à l'oignon
onion soup

spécialités régionales
regional specialities

sucre
sugar

thon
tuna

thym
thyme

tripes
tripe

truffes
truffles

truite
trout

truite saumonée
salmon trout

turbot
turbot

vapeur (à la)
steamed

venaison
venison

viande hachée
minced meat/mince

vin blanc
white wine

vin rosé
rosé wine

vin rouge
red wine

vinaigre
vinegar

xérès
sherry

5. On the road

5.1 Asking for directions

Excuse me, could I ask
you something?

Pardon, puis-je vous demander
quelque chose?
*pahrdawn, pwee jhuh voo duhmohnday
kehlkuh shoaz?*

I've lost my way.

Je me suis égaré(e).
jhuh muh swee zaygahray

Is there an... around here?

Connaissez-vous un...dans les environs?
*konehssay voo zuhn... dohn lay
zohnveerawn?*

Is this the way to...?

Est-ce la route vers...?
ehs lah root vehr...?

Could you tell me how
to get to...?

Pouvez-vous me dire comment aller à...?
*poovay voo muh deer komohn
tahlay ah...?*

What's the quickest way to...?

Comment puis-je arriver le plus vite
possible à...?
*komohn pwee jhuh ahreevay luh plew
veet pohseebl ah...?*

How many kilometres
is it to...?

Il y a encore combien de kilomètres
jusqu'à...?
*eel ee yah ohnkor kohnbyahn duh
keeloamehtr jhewskah...?*

**Je ne sais pas, je ne suis
pas d'ici.**

I don't know, I don't know my way
around here.

Vous vous êtes trompé.

You're going the wrong way.

**Vous devez retourner à...Là-bas
les panneaux vous indiqueront
la route.**

You have to go back to... From
there on just follow the signs.

**Là-bas vous demanderez à
nouveau votre route.**

When you get there, ask again.

Could you point it out on the map?	*Pouvez-vous me l'indiquer sur la carte?* *poovay voo muh lahndeekay sewr lah kahrt?*	

tout droit straight ahead	**le feu (de signalisation)** the traffic light	**le pont** the bridge
à gauche left	**le tunnel** the tunnel	**le passage à niveau** the level crossing
à droite right	**le panneau `cédez la priorité'** the `give way' sign	**la barrière** boom
tourner turn	**l'immeuble** the building	**le panneau direction...** the sign pointing to...
suivre follow	**à l'angle, au coin** at the corner	**la flèche** the arrow
traverser cross	**la rivière, le fleuve** the river	
le carrefour the intersection	**l'autopont** the fly-over	
la rue the street		

5.2 Customs

● When bringing your car into France along with your passport you must carry your original documents with you. These include your valid full driving licence (together with paper counterpart if photocard licence), vehicle registration document and motor insurance certificate. Contact your motor insurer for advice at least a month before taking your vehicle overseas to ensure that you are adequately covered. It is advisable to carry a fire extinguisher and first-aid kit. It is compulsory to carry a warning triangle, a reflective jacket (EN471) and a breathalyser. Entry regulations can change at very short notice, so you are advised to check with your travel agent, airline, ferry or rail company that you have the correct documentation before your journey.

For further information see www.theaa.com/driving-advice/driving-abroad

Votre passeport s'il vous plaît.	Your passport, please.
La carte verte s'il vous plaît.	Your green card, please.
La carte grise s'il vous plaît.	Your vehicle documents, please.
Votre visa s'il vous plaît.	Your visa, please.
Où allez-vous?	Where are you heading?
Combien de temps pensez-vous rester?	How long are you planning to stay?
Avez-vous quelque chose à déclarer?	Do you have anything to declare?
Voulez-vous l'ouvrir?	Open this, please.

I'm travelling through.
Je suis de passage.
jhuh swee duh pahsahjh

I'm going on holiday to...
Je vais en vacances en...
jhuh veh zohn vahkohns ohn...

I'm on a business trip.
Je suis en voyage d'affaires.
jhuh swee zohn vwahyahjh dahfehr

I don't know how long I'll be staying yet.
Je ne sais pas encore combien de temps je reste.
jhuh nuh seh pah zohnkor kawnbyahn duh tohn jhuh rehst

I'll be staying here for a weekend.
Je reste un week-end ici.
jhuh rehst uhn weekehnd eesee

– for a few days.
Je reste quelques jours ici.
jhuh rehst kehlkuh jhoor eesee

– for a week.
Je reste une semaine ici.
jhuh rehst ewn suhmehn eesee

– for two weeks.
Je reste quinze jours ici.
jhuh rehst kahnz jhoor eesee

I've got nothing to declare.
Je n'ai rien à déclarer.
jhuh nay ryahn nah dayklahray

I've got...with me.
J'ai... avec moi.
jhay... ahvehk mwah

– cartons of cigarettes...	J'ai des cartouches de cigarettes...
	jhay day kahrtoosh duh seegahreht...
– bottles of...	J'ai des bouteilles de...
	jhay day bootehy duh...
– some souvenirs...	J'ai quelques souvenirs...
	jhay kehlkuh soovneer...
These are personal effects.	Ce sont des affaires personnelles.
	suh sawn day zahfehr pehrsonehl
These are not new.	Ces affaires ne sont pas neuves.
	say zahfehr nuh sawn pah nuhv
Here's the receipt.	Voici la facture.
	vwahsee lah fahktewr
This is for private use.	C'est pour usage personnel.
	seh poor ewzahjh pehrsonehl
How much import duty do I have to pay?	Combien de droits d'importation dois-je payer?
	kawnbyahn duh drwah dahnpohrtasyawn dwah jhuh payay?
Can I go now?	Puis-je partir maintenant?
	pwee jhuh pahrteer mahntuhnohn?

5.3 Luggage

Porter!	Porteur!
	portuhr!
Could you take this luggage to...?	Voulez-vous porter ces bagages à... s'il vous plaît?
	voolay voo portay say bahgahjh ah... seel voo pleh?
How much do I owe you?	Combien vous dois-je?
	kawnbyahn voo dwah jhuh?
Where can I find a luggage trolley?	Où puis-je trouver un chariot pour les bagages?
	oo pwee jhuh troovay uhn shahryoa poor lay bahgahjh?

Could you store this luggage for me?	Puis-je mettre ces bagages en consigne?
	pwee jhuh mehtr say bahgahjh ohn kawnseenyuh?
Where are the luggage lockers?	Où est la consigne automatique?
	oo eh lah kawnseenyuh oatoamahteek?
I can't get the locker open.	Je n'arrive pas à ouvrir la consigne.
	jhuh nahreev pah zah oovreer lah kawnseenyuh
How much is it per item per day?	Combien cela coûte-t-il par bagage par jour?
	kawnbyahn suhlah koot-uh teel pahr bahgahjh pahr jhoor?
This is not my bag/suitcase.	Ce n'est pas mon sac/ma valise.
	suh neh pah mawn sahk/mah vahleez
There's one item/bag/ suitcase missing still.	Il manque encore une chose/un sac/ une valise.
	eel mohnk ohnkor ewn shoaz/uhn sahk/ ewn vahleez
My suitcase is damaged.	Ma valise est abîmée.
	mah vahleez eh tahbeemay

5.4 Traffic signs

accès interdit à tous les véhicules
no entry

accotement non stabilisé
soft verge

allumez vos feux
switch on lights

autoroute
motorway

barrière de dégel
road closed

bison fûté
recommended route

brouillard fréquent
beware fog

cédez le passage
give way

chaussée à gravillons
loose chippings

chaussée déformée
uneven road surface

chaussée glissante
slippery road

circulation alternée
alternate priority

danger
danger

carrefour dangereux
dangerous crossing

**danger priorité
à droite**
priority to vehicles
from right

**descente
dangereuse**
steep hill

déviation
diversion

fin de...
end of...

**fin d'allumage
des feux**
end of need
for lights

fin de chantier
end of road works

**interdiction
de dépasser**
no overtaking

**interdiction
de klaxonner**
no horns

**interdiction sauf
riverains**
access only

limite de vitesse
speed limit

passage à niveau
level crossing

passage d'animaux
animals crossing

**passage pour
piétons**
pedestrian crossing

péage
toll

poids lourds
heavy goods vehicles

rappel
reminder

**remorques et
semi-remorques**
lorries and
articulated lorries

sens unique
one-way traffic

serrez à droite
keep right

sortie
exit

sortie de camions
factory/works exit

**interdiction de
stationner**
no parking

taxis
taxi rank

travaux (sur...km)
roadworks ahead

véhicules lents
slow traffic

**véhicules
transportant
des matières
dangereuses**
vehicles transporting
dangerous
substances

verglas fréquent
ice on road

virages sur...km
bends for...km

vitesse limite
maximum speed

zone bleue
parking disc required

zone piétonne
pedestrian zone

5.5 The car

● **Particular traffic regulations:**

Maximum speed for cars:

Motorways: 130 km/h; 110 km/h in wet conditions

Dual carriageways: 110 km/h; 100 km/h in wet conditions.

Main roads: 80 km/h; 70 km/h in wet conditions.

Built-up areas, like towns and cities: 50 km/h, unless otherwise indicated.

It is recommended that all vehicles use dipped headlights day
and night outside built-up areas.

The parts of a car

battery	**la batterie**	*lah bahtree*
rear light	**le feu arrière**	*luh fuh ahryehr*
rear-view mirror	**le rétroviseur**	*luh raytroaveezuhr*
reversing light	**le phare de recul**	*luh fahr duh ruhkewl*
aerial	**l'antenne (f.)**	*lohntehn*
car radio	**l'autoradio (m.)**	*loatoarahdyoa*
petrol tank	**le réservoir d'essence**	*luh rayzehrvwahr dehssohns*
inside mirror	**le rétroviseur intérieur**	*luh raytroaveezuhr ahntayryuhr*
sparking plugs	**les bougies (f.)**	*llay boojhee*
fuel filter/pump	**le filtre à carburant/ la pompe à carburant**	*luh feeltr ah kahrbewrohn/ lah pawnp ah kahrbewrohn*
wing mirror	**le rétroviseur de côté**	*luh raytroaveezuhr duh koatay*
bumper	**le pare-chocs**	*luh pahr shok*
carburettor	**le carburateur**	*luh kahrbewrahtuhr*
crankcase	**le carter**	*lluh kahrtehr*
cylinder	**le cylindre**	*luh seelahndr*

ignition	l'allumage	l'ahlewmahjh
warning light	la lampe témoin	lah lohnp taymwahn
dynamo	la dynamo	lah deenahmoa
accelerator	l'accélérateur	lahksaylayrahtuhr
handbrake	le frein à main	luh frahn ah mahn
valve	la soupape	lah soopahp
silencer	le silencieux	luh seelohnsyuh
boot	le coffre	luh kofr
headlight	le phare	luh fahr
crank shaft	le vilebrequin	luh veelbruhkahn
air filter	le filtre à air	luh feeltr ah ehr
fog lamp	le phare anti-brouillar	luh fahr ohntee brooy-yahr
engine block	le bloc moteur	luh blok motuhr
camshaft	l'arbre à cames	lahrbr ah kahm
oil filter/pump	le filtre à huile/ la pompe à huile	luh feeltr ah weel/ lah pawnp ah weel
dipstick	la jauge du niveau d'huile	lah jhoajh dew neevoa dweel
pedal	la pédale	lah paydahl
door	la portière	lah portyehr
radiator	le radiateur	luh rahdyahtuhr
disc brake	le frein à disque	luh frahn ah deesk
spare wheel	la roue de secours	lah roo duh suhkoor
indicator	le clignotant	luh kleenyohtohn
windscreen wiper	l'essuie-glace (m.)	lehswee glahs
shock absorbers	les amortisseurs (m.)	lay zahmorteesuhr
sunroof	le toit ouvrant	luh twah oovrohn
starter motor	le démarreur	luh daymahruhr
steering column	la colonne de direction	lah kolon duh deerehksyawn
steering wheel	le volant	luh volohn
exhaust pipe	le tuyau d'échappement	luh tweeyoa dayshahpmohn

seat belt	la ceinture de sécurité	*lah sahntewr duh saykewreetay*
fan	le ventilateur	*luh vohnteelahtuhr*
distributor cable	le câble distributeur	*luh kahbl deestreebewtuhr*
gear lever	le levier de vitesses	*luh luhvyay duh veetehs*
windscreen	le pare-brise	*luh pahrbreez*
water pump	la pompe à eau	*lah pawnp ah oa*
wheel	la roue	*lah roo*
hubcap	l'enjoliveur	*lohnjholeevuhr*
piston	le piston	*luh peestawn*

5.6 The petrol station

How many kilometres to the next petrol station, please?	Il y a combien de kilomètres jusqu'à la prochaine station-service? *eel ee yah kawnbyahn duh keeloamehtr jhewskah lah proshehn stasyawn sehrvees?*
I would like...litres of..., please.	Je voudrais ... litres. *jhuh voodreh ... leetr*
– 4-star	Je voudrais ... litres de super. *jhuh voodreh ... leetr duh sewpehr*
– leaded	Je voudrais ... litres d'essence ordinaire. *jhuh voodreh ... leetr dehssohns ohrdeenehr*
– unleaded	Je voudrais ... litres d'essence sans plomb. *jhuh voodreh ... leetr dehssohns sohn plawn*
– diesel	Je voudrais ... litres de gazoil. *jhuh voodreh ... leetr duh gahzwahl*

I would like... euros worth of petrol, please.	Je voudrais pour ... Euro d'essence s'il vous plaît.
	jhuh voodreh poor ... Euro dehssohns seel voo pleh
Fill it up, please.	Le plein s'il vous plaît.
	luh plahn seel voo pleh
Could you check...?	Vous voulez contrôler...?
	voo voolay kawntroalay...?
– the oil level	Vous voulez contrôler le niveau d'huile?
	voo voolay kawntroalay luh neevoa dweel?
– the tyre pressure	Vous voulez contrôler la pression des pneus?
	voo voolay kawntroalay lah prehsyawn day pnuh?
Could you change the oil, please?	Vous pouvez changer l'huile?
	voo poovay shohnjhay lweel?
Could you clean the windows/the windscreen, please?	Vous pouvez nettoyer les vitres/le pare-brise?
	voo poovay nehtwahhay lay veetr/luh pahrbreez?
Could you give the car a wash, please?	Vous pouvez faire laver la voiture?
	voo poovay fehr lahvay lah vwahtewr?

5.7 Breakdown and repairs

I'm having car trouble. Could you give me a hand?	Je suis en panne. Vous pouvez m'aider?
	jhuh swee zohn pahnn. voo poovay mayday?
I've run out of petrol.	Je n'ai plus d'essence.
	jhuh neh plew dehssohns
I've locked the keys in the car.	J'ai laissé les clefs dans la voiture fermée.
	jhay layssay lay klay dohn lah vwahtewr fehrmay

The car/motorbike/ moped won't start.	La voiture/la moto/le vélomoteur ne démarre pas.
	lah vwahtewr/lah moatoa/luh vayloamotuhr nuh daymahr pah
Could you contact the recovery service for me, please?	Vous pouvez m'appeler l'assistance routière?
	voo poovay mahpuhlay lahseestohns rootyehr?
Could you call a garage for me, please?	Vous pouvez m'appeler un garage?
	voo poovay mahpuhlay uhn gahrahjh?
Could you give me a lift to...?	Puis-je aller avec vous jusqu'à ...?
	pwee jhahlay ahvehk voo jhewskah ...?
– a garage/into town?	Puis-je aller avec vous jusqu'à un garage/la ville?
	pwee jhahlay ahvehk voo jhewskah uhn gahrahjh/lah veel?
– a phone booth?	Puis-je aller avec vous jusqu'à une cabine téléphonique?
	pwee jhahlay ahvehk voo jhewskah ewn kahbeen taylayfoneek?
– an emergency phone?	Puis-je aller avec vous jusqu'à un téléphone d'urgence?
	pwee jhalay ahvehk voo jhewskah uhn taylayfon dewrjhohns?
Can we take my bicycle/ moped?	Est-ce que vous pouvez également prendre mon vélo(moteur)?
	ehs kuh voo poovay aygahlmohn prohndr mawn vayloa(motuhr)?
Could you tow me to a garage?	Vous pouvez me remorquer jusqu'à un garage?
	voo poovay muh ruhmorkay jhewskah uhn gahrahjh?
There's probably something wrong with...*(See page 76)*	Le ... a certainement quelque chose de défectueux.
	luh ... ah sehrtehnemohn kehlkuh shoaz duh dayfehktewuh

Can you fix it?	Vous pouvez le réparer?
	voo poovay luh raypahray?
Could you fix my tyre?	Vous pouvez réparer mon pneu?
	voo poovay raypahray mawn pnuh?
Could you change this wheel?	Vous pouvez changer cette roue?
	voo poovay shohnjhay seht roo?
Can you fix it so it'll get me to...?	Vous pouvez le réparer pour que je puisse rouler jusqu'à...?
	voo poovay luh raypahray poor kuh jhuh pwees roolay jhewskah...?
Which garage can help me?	Quel garage pourrait m'aider?
	kehl gahrahjh pooreh mayday?
When will my car/bicycle be ready?	Quand est-ce que ma voiture/ma bicyclette sera prête?
	kohn tehs kuh mah vwahtewr/mah beeseekleht suhrah preht?
Can I wait for it here?	Je peux l'attendre ici?
	jhuh puh lahtohndr eesee?
How much will it cost?	Combien cela va coûter?
	kawnbyahn suhlah vah kootay?
Could you itemise the bill?	Vous pouvez me détailler la note?
	voo poovay muh daytahyay lah not?
Can I have a receipt for the insurance?	Puis-je avoir un reçu pour l'assurance?
	pwee jhahvwahr uhn ruhsew poor lahsewrohns?

5.8 The bicycle/moped

● Cycle paths are rare in France. Bikes can be hired at tourist centres (*vélo tout terrain* = mountain bike). Not much consideration for bikes should be expected on the roads. The maximum speed for mopeds is 45km/h both inside and outside town centres. A helmet is compulsory.

The parts of a bicycle

rear lamp	le feu arrière	*luh fuh ahryehr*
rear wheel	la roue arrière	*lah roo ahryehr*
(luggage) carrier	le porte-bagages	*luh port bahgahjh*
bicycle fork	la tête de fourche	*lah teht duh foorsh*
bell	la sonnette	*lah sohneht*
inner tube	la chambre à air	*lah shohnbr ah ehr*
tyre	le pneu	*luh pnuh*
crank	le pédalier	*luh paydahlyay*
gear change	le changement de vitesse	*luh shohnjhmohn duh veetehs*
wire	le fil (électrique)	*luh feel (aylehktreek)*
dynamo	la dynamo	*lah deenahmoa*
bicycle trailer	la remorque de bicyclette	*lah ruhmork duh beeseekleht*
frame	le cadre	*luh kahdr*
dress guard	le protège-jupe	*luh protehjh jhewp*
chain	la chaîne	*lah shehn*
chainguard	le carter	*luh kahrtehr*
padlock	l'antivol (m.)	*lohnteevol*
milometer	le compteur kilométrique	*luh kawntuhr keeloamaytreek*
child's seat	le siège-enfant	*luh syehjh ohnfohn*
headlamp	le phare	*luh fahr*
bulb	l'ampoule (f.)	*lohnpool*
pedal	la pédale	*lah paydahl*

pump	la pompe	*lah pawnp*
reflector	le réflecteur	*luh rayflehktuhr*
break blocks	les patins	*lay pahtahn*
brake cable	le câble de frein	*luh kahbl duh frahn*
wheel lock	le cadenas pour bicyclette	*lah kaduhnah poor beeseekleht*
carrier straps	le tendeur	*luh tohnduhr*
tachometer	le compteur de vitesse	*luh kawntuhr duh veetehs*
spoke	le rayon	*luh rayawn*
mudguard	le garde-boue	*luh gahrd boo*
handlebar	le guidon	*luh gueedawn*
chain wheel	le pignon	*luh peenyawn*
toe clip	le câle-pied	*luh kahl pyay*
crank axle	l'axe du pédalier (m.)	*lahx dew paydahlyay*
drum brake	le frein à tambour	*luh frahn ah tohnboor*
rim	la jante	*lah jhohnt*
valve	la valve	*lah vahlv*
valve tube	le raccord souple de la valve	*luh rahkor soopl duh lah vahlv*
gear cable	la chaîne du dérailleur	*lah shehn dew dayrahyuhr*
fork	la fourche	*lah foorsh*
front wheel	la roue avant	*lah roo ahvohn*
saddle	la selle	*lah sehl*

Je n'ai pas les pièces détachées pour votre voiture/bicyclette.	I don't have parts for your car/bicycle.
Je dois aller chercher les pièces détachées ailleurs.	I have to get the parts from somewhere else.
Je dois commander les pièces détachées.	I have to order the parts.
Cela prendra une demi-journée.	That'll take half a day.
Cela prendra une journée.	That'll take a day.
Cela prendra quelques jours.	That'll take a few days.
Cela prendra une semaine.	That'll take a week.
Votre voiture est bonne pour la ferraille.	Your car is a write-off.
Il n'y a plus rien à y faire.	It can't be repaired.
La voiture/la moto/la mobylette/ la bicyclette sera prête à... heures.	The car/motor bike/moped/bicycle will be ready at... o'clock.

5.9 Renting a vehicle

I'd like to rent a...
J'aimerais louer un...
jhehmuhreh looay uhn...

Do I need a (special) licence for that?
Me faut-il un permis spécial?
muh foa teel uhn pehrmee spaysyal?

I'd like to rent the...for...
Je voudrais louer le/la...pour
jhuh voodreh looay luh/lah...poor

– one day
Je voudrais louer le/la...pour une journée.
jhuh voodreh looay luh/lah...poor ewn jhoornay

two days	Je voodreh louer le/la...pour deux jours.
	jhuh voodreh looay luh/lah...poor duh jhoor
How much is that per day/week?	C'est combien par jour/semaine?
	seh kawnbyahn pahr jhoor/suhmehn?
How much is the deposit?	De combien est la caution?
	duh kawnbyahn eh lah koasyawn?
Could I have a receipt for the deposit?	Puis-je avoir un reçu pour la caution?
	pwee jhahvwahr uhn ruhsew poor lah koasyawn?
How much is the surcharge per kilometre?	Quel est le supplément par kilomètre?
	kehl eh luh sewplaymohn pahr keeloamehtr?
Does that include petrol?	Est-ce que l'essence est incluse?
	ehs kuh lehsohns eh tahnklewz?
Does that include insurance?	Est-ce que l'assurance est incluse?
	ehs kuh lahsewrohns eh tahnklewz?
What time can I pick the... up tomorrow?	Demain, à quelle heure puis-je venir chercher la...?
	duhmahn ah kehl uhr pwee jhuh vuhneer shehrshay lah...?
When does the...have to be back?	Quand dois-je rapporter la...?
	kohn dwah jhuh rahportay lah...?
Where's the petrol tank?	Où est le réservoir?
	oo eh luh rayzehrvwahr?
What sort of fuel does it take?	Quel carburant faut-il utiliser?
	kehl kahrbewrohn foa teel ewteeleezay?

6. Public transport

● You can check departure times by telephone or on the internet. Tickets for buses and the *métro* (Paris, Lyon and Marseille) are cheaper when bought in a *carnet* (book of ten), available at kiosks near some bus stops, at newsagents and in *métro* stations.

Announcements

☞

Le train de...heures, en direction de... a un retard de... minutes.	The...train to...has been delayed by...minutes.
Le train en direction de.../en provenance de...arrive sur le quai...	The train now arriving at platform... is the...train to .../from...
Le train en direction de...va quitter le quai...dans quelques instants.	The train to...is about to leave from platform...
Attention éloignez-vous de la voie, un train rapide va passer sur la voie...	Attention please, keep your distance from the rail track, an intercity train will pass on platform...
Nous approchons la gare de...	We're now approaching...

Where does this train go to?	Où va ce train?
	oo vah suh trahn?
Does this boat go to...?	Ce bateau, va-t-il à...?
	suh bahtoa, vah teel ah...?
Can I take this bus to...?	Puis-je prendre ce bus pour aller à...?
	pwee jhuh prondr suh bews poor ahlay ah...?
Does this train stop at...?	Ce train s'arrête-t-il à...?
	suh trahn sahreht-uh-teel ah...?

Is this seat taken/free/
reserved?

Est-ce que cette place est occupée/
 libre/réservée?

*ehs kuh seht plahs eh tokewpay/leebr/
 rayzehrvay?*

I've booked...

J'ai réservé...

jhay rayzehrvay...

Could you tell me where
 I have to get off for...?

Voulez-vous me dire où descendre
 pour...?

*voolay voo muh deer oo duhsohndr
 poor...?*

Could you let me know when
 we get to...?

Voulez-me prévenir lorsque nous
 serons à...?

*voolay voo muh prayvuhneer lorskuh noo
 suhrawn zah...?*

Could you stop at the next
 stop, please?

Voulez-vous vous arrêter au prochain
 arrêt s'il vous plaît?

*voolay voo voo zahrehtay oa proshahn
 nahreht seel voo pleh?*

Where are we now?

Où sommes-nous ici?

oo som noo zeesee?

Do I have to get off here?

Dois-je descendre ici?

dwah jhuh duhsohndr eesee?

Have we already passed...?

Avons-nous déjà dépassé...?

ahvawn noo dayjhah daypahsay...?

How long have I been asleep?

Combien de temps ai-je dormi?

kawnbyahn duh tohn ay jhuh dormee?

How long does...stop here?

Combien de temps...reste ici?

kawnbyahn duh tohn...rehst eesee?

Can I come back on the
 same ticket?

Puis-je revenir avec ce billet?

*pwee jhuh ruhvuhneer ahvehk
 suh beeyeh?*

Can I change on this ticket?

Puis-je prendre une correspondance
 avec ce billet?

*pwee jhuh prondr ewn korehspawndohns
 ahvehk suh beeyeh?*

How long is this ticket valid for?	Combien de temps ce billet reste-t-il valable?
	kawnbyahn duh tohn suh beeyeh rehst-uh-teel vahlahbl?
How much is the supplement for the TGV (high speed train)?	Combien coûte le supplément pour le TGV?
	kawnbyahn koot luh sewplaymohn poor luh tayjhayvay?

6.2 Questions to passengers

Ticket types

Première classe ou deuxième classe?	First or second class?
Aller simple ou retour?	Single or return?
Fumeurs ou non fumeurs?	Smoking or non-smoking?
Côté fenêtre ou côté couloir?	Window or aisle?
A l'avant ou à l'arrière?	Front or back?
Place assise ou couchette?	Seat or couchette?
Au-dessus, au milieu ou au-dessous?	Top, middle or bottom?
Classe touriste ou classe affaires?	Tourist class or business class?
Une cabine ou un fauteuil?	Cabin or seat?
Une personne ou deux personnes?	Single or double?
Vous êtes combien de personnes à voyager?	How many are travelling?

Destination

Où allez-vous?	Where are you travelling?
Quand partez-vous?	When are you leaving?
Votre...part à...	Your...leaves at...
Vous devez prendre une correspondance.	You have to change trains.
Vous devez descendre à...	You have to get off at...
Vous devez passer par...	You have to travel via...
L'aller est le...	The outward journey is on...
Le retour est le...	The return journey is on...
Vous devez être à bord au plus tard à...	You have to be on board by...

Votre billet s'il vous plaît.	Your ticket, please.
Votre réservation s'il vous plaît.	Your reservation, please.
Votre passeport s'il vous plaît.	Your passport, please.
Vous n'êtes pas à la bonne place.	You're in the wrong seat.
Vous êtes dans le mauvais...	You're on/in the wrong...
Cette place est réservée.	This seat is reserved.
Vous devez payer un supplément.	You'll have to pay a supplement.
Le...a un retard de...minutes.	The...has been delayed by... minutes.

6.3 Tickets

Where can I...?	Où puis-je...?
	oo pwee jhuh...?
buy a ticket?	Où puis-je acheter un billet?
	oo pwee jhahshtay uhn beeyeh?
make a reservation?	Où puis-je réserver une place?
	oo pwee jhuh rayzehrvay ewn plahs?
book a flight?	Où puis-je réserver un vol?
	oo pwee jhuh rayzehrvay uhn vol?
Could I have a...to..., please?	Puis-je avoir...en direction de...?
	pwee jhahvwahr...ohn deerehksyawn duh...?
a single?	Puis-je avoir un aller simple?
	pwee jhahvwahr uhn nahlay sahnpl?
a return?	Puis-je avoir un aller-retour?
	pwee jhahvwahr uhn nahlay ruhtoor?
first class	première classe
	pruhmyehr klahs
second class	deuxième classe
	duhzyehm klahs
tourist class	classe touriste
	klahs tooreest
business class	classe affaires
	klahs ahfehr
I'd like to book a seat/ couchette/cabin.	Je voudrais réserver une place assise/ couchette/cabine.
	jhuh voodreh rayzehrvay ewn plahs ahseez/koosheht/kahbeen
I'd like to book a berth in the sleeping car.	Je voudrais réserver une place dans le wagon-lit.
	jhuh voodreh rayzehrvay ewn plahs dohn luh vahgawnlee

top/middle/bottom	au-dessus/au milieu/au-dessous
	oaduhsew/oa meelyuh/oa duhsoo
smoking/no smoking	fumeurs/non fumeurs
	fewmuhr/nawn fewmuhr
by the window	à côté de la fenêtre
	ah koatay duh lah fenehtr
single/double	une personne/deux personnes
	ewn pehrson/duh pehrson
at the front/back	à l'avant/à l'arrière
	ah lahvohn/ah lahryehr
There are...of us.	Nous sommes...personnes.
	noo som...pehrson
a car	une voiture
	ewn vwahtewr
a caravan	une caravane
	ewn kahrahvahnn
...bicycles	...bicyclettes
	...beeseekleht
Do you also have...?	Avez-vous aussi...?
	ahvay voo zoasee...?
– season tickets?	Avez-vous aussi une carte d'abonnement?
	ahvay voo zoasee ewn kahrt dahbonmohn?
– weekly tickets?	Avez-vous aussi une carte hebdomadaire?
	ahvay voo zoasee ewn kahrt ehbdomahdehr?
– monthly season tickets?	Avez-vous aussi une carte mensuelle?
	ahvay voo zoasee ewn kahrt mohnsewehl?

Where's...?	Où se trouve...?
	oo suh troov...?
Where's the information desk?	Où se trouve le bureau de renseignements?
	oo suh troov luh bewroa duh rohnsehnyuhmohn?
Where can I find a timetable?	Où se trouvent les horaires des départs/des arrivées?
	oo se troov lay zorehr day daypahr/day zahreevay?
Where's the...desk?	Où se trouve la réception de...?
	oo se troov lah raysehpsyawn duh...?
Do you have a city map with the bus/the underground routes on it?	Avez-vous un plan du réseau des bus/du métro?
	ahvay voo zuhn plohn dew rayzoa day bews/dew maytroa?
Do you have a timetable?	Avez-vous un horaire des arrivées et des départs?
	ahvay voo zuhn norehr day zahreevay ay day daypahr?
I'd like to confirm/cancel/change my booking for...	Je veux confirmer/annuler/changer ma réservation pour...
	jhuh vuh kawnfeermay/ahnewlay/shohnjhay mah rayzehrvahsyawn poor...
Will I get my money back?	Mon argent me sera rendu?
	mawn nahrjhohn muh suhrah rohndew?
I want to go to...How do I get there? (What's the quickest way there?)	Je dois aller à...Comment puis-je y aller (le plus vite possible)?
	jhuh dwah zahlay ah...komohn pwee jhee ahlay (luh plew veet poseebl)?

How much is a single/
  return to...?
Combien coûte un aller simple/un
  aller-retour pour...?
*kawnbyahn koot uhn nahlay sahnpl/uhn
  nahlay retoor poor...?*

Do I have to pay
  a supplement?
Dois-je payer un supplément?
dwah jheuh payay uhn sewplaymohn?

Can I interrupt my journey
  with this ticket?
Puis-je interrompre mon voyage
  avec ce billet?
*pwee jhahntayrawnpr mawn vwahyahjh
  ahvehk suh beeyeh?*

How much luggage
  am I allowed?
J'ai droit à combien de bagages?
jhay drwah ah kawnbyahn duh bahgahjh?

Does this...travel direct?
Ce...est direct?
suh...eh deerehkt?

Do I have to change? Where?
Dois-je changer? Où?
dwah jhuh shohnjhay? oo?

Will this plane make
  any stopovers?
L'avion fait escale?
lahvyawn feh tehskahl?

Does the boat call in at any
  ports on the way?
Est-ce que le bateau fait escale dans
  un port pendant son trajet?
*ehs kuh luh bahtoa feh tehskahl dohn
  zuhn por pohndohn sawn trahjheh?*

Does the train/bus stop at...?
Est-ce que le train/le bus s'arrête à...?
ehs kuh luh trahn/luh bews sahreht ah...?

Where should I get off?
Où dois-je descendre?
oo dwah jhuh duhsohndr?

Is there a connection to...?
Y a-t-il une correspondance pour...?
*ee yah teel ewn korehspawndohns
  poor...?*

How long do I have to wait?
Combien de temps dois-je attendre?
kawnbyahn duh tohn dwah jhahtohndr?

When does...leave?
Quand part...?
kohn pahr...?

What time does the first/ next/last...leave?	A quelle heure part le premier/ prochain/dernier...? *ah kehl uhr pahr luh pruhmyay/proshahn/ dehrnyay...?*
How long does...take?	Combien de temps met le...? *kawnbyahn duh tohn meh luh...?*
What time does...arrive in...?	A quelle heure arrive...à...? *ah kehl uhr ahreev...ah...?*
Where does the...to... leave from?	D'où part le...pour...? *doo pahr luh...poor...?*
Is this...to...?	Est-ce le...pour...? *ehs luh...poor...?*

6.5 Aeroplanes

● At arrival at a French airport (*aéroport*), you will find the following signs:

arrivée arrivals	**départ** departures

6.6 Trains

The rail network is extensive. *La Société Nationale des Chemins de Fer Français (SNCF)* is responsible for the national rail traffic. Besides the normal train, there is also *le Train à Grande Vitesse (TGV)* for which you will have to pay a supplement. Reservations before departure are cheaper. The TGV operates between the larger cities: Paris, Lyon, Marseille and Nice. A train ticket has to be stamped (*composté*) before departure.

● In nearly all large cities, there are plenty of taxis. French taxis have no fixed colour. Virtually all taxis have a meter. In the smaller towns, it is usual to agree a fixed price in advance. A supplement is usual for luggage, a journey at night, on a Sunday or Bank holiday, or to an airport. It is advisable in large cities such as Paris and Lyon to check that the meter has been returned to zero at the start of the journey.

libre	occupé	station de taxis
for hire	booked	taxi rank

Taxi!	Taxi!
	tahksee!
Could you get me a taxi, please?	Pouvez-vous m'appeler un taxi?
	poovay voo mahpuhlay uhn tahksee?
Where can I find a taxi around here?	Où puis-je prendre un taxi par ici?
	oo pwee jhuh prohndr uhn tahksee pahr eesee?
Could you take me to…, please?	Conduisez-moi à…s'il vous plaît.
	kawndweezay mwah ah…seel voo pleh
– this address.	Conduisez-moi à cette adresse.
	kawndweezay mwah ah seht ahdrehs
– the…hotel.	Conduisez-moi à l'hôtel…
	kawndweezay mwah ah loatehl…
– the town/city centre.	Conduisez-moi dans le centre.
	kawndweezay mwah dohn luh sohntr
– the station.	Conduisez-moi à la gare.
	kawndweezay mwah ah lah gahr
– the airport.	Conduisez-moi à l'aéroport.
	kawndweezay mwah ah layroapor.
How much is the trip to…?	Combien coûte un trajet jusqu'à…?
	kawnbyahn koot uhn trahjheh jhewskah…?

How far is it to...?	C'est combien de kilomètres jusqu'à...?
	seh kawnbyahn duh keeloamehtr jhewskah...?
Could you turn on the meter, please?	Voulez-vous mettre le compteur en marche s'il vous plaît?
	voolay voo mehtr luh kawntuhr ohn mahrsh seel voo pleh?
I'm in a hurry.	Je suis pressé.
	jhuh swee prehssay
Could you speed up/slow down a little?	Vous pouvez rouler plus vite/plus lentement?
	voo poovay roolay plew veet/plew lohntmohn?
Could you take a different route?	Vous pouvez prendre une autre route?
	voo poovay prohndr ewn oatr root?
I'd like to get out here, please.	Je voudrais descendre ici.
	jhuh voodreh duhsohndr eesee
You have to go...here.	Là vous allez...
	lah voo zahlay...
You have to go straight on here.	Là vous allez tout droit.
	lah voo zahlay too drwah
You have to turn left here.	Là vous allez à gauche.
	lah voo zahlay zah goash
You have to turn right here.	Là vous allez à droite.
	lah voo zahlay zah drwaht
This is it.	C'est ici.
	seht eesee
Could you wait a minute for me, please?	Vous pouvez m'attendre un instant?
	voo poovay mahtohndr uhn nahnstohn?

7. Overnight accommodation

● There is great variety of overnight accommodation in France.
Hôtels: stars indicate the degree of comfort; from five stars, the most luxurious, to one star, very simple. Beside the star one often finds the letters NN-*Nouvelles Normes* (new classifications). This means that the star-classification is up-to-date. Most hotels offer *pension complète* (full board) or *demi-pension* (half board).
Auberges et Relais de campagne: luxurious; splendid view and lots of rest are guaranteed.
Châteaux, Hôtels de France and Vieilles Demeures: a very expensive tourist residence, always within a castle, country manor or an historic building.
Logis de France: an organisation with many hotels with one or two stars, mostly outside the town centre. The hotel can be recognised by the yellow signboards with a green fireplace and the words: *logis de France.*
Motels: especially along the motorway, comparable to UK motels.
Auberges de jeunesse (youth hostel): the number of nights is restricted to between three and seven.
Camping: free camping is allowed, except for forest areas with the sign *attention au feu* (fire hazard). Not all camping sites are guarded.
Refuges et gîtes d'étape (mountain huts): in the Alps and Pyrenees. These huts are owned by the *Club Alpin Français* and are inexpensive.

Combien de temps voulez-vous rester?	How long do you want to stay?
Voulez-vous remplir ce questionnaire s'il vous plaît?	Fill out this form, please.
Puis-je avoir votre passeport?	Could I see your passport?
J'ai besoin de vos informations de carte de crédit.	I'll need your credit card details.
Vous devez payer un acompte.	I'll need a deposit.
Vous devez payer à l'avance.	You'll have to pay in advance.

My name's...I've made a reservation over the phone/by mail/online.

Mon nom est...J'ai réservé une place par téléphone/par lettre/en ligne/sur Internet.

mawn nawn eh...jhay rayzehrvay ewn plahs pahr taylayfon/pahr lehtr/ohn leenyuh/sewr ahntehrneht

How much is it per night/week/month?

Quel est le prix pour une nuit/une semaine/un mois?

kehl eh luh pree poor ewn nwee/ewn suhmehn/uhn mwah?

We'll be staying at least... nights/weeks.

Nous restons au moins...nuits/semaines.

noo rehstawn zoa mwhan...nwee/suhmehn

We don't know yet.

Nous ne le savons pas encore exactement.

noo nuh luh sahvawn pah zohnkor ehgzahktmohn

Do you allow pets (cats/dogs)?

Est-ce que les animaux domestiques (chiens/chats) sont admis?

ehs kuh lay zahneemoa domehsteek (shyahn/shah) sawn tahdmee?

What time does the gate/door open/close?

A quelle heure on ouvre/ferme le portail/la porte?

ah keh uhr awn noovr/fehrm luh portahy/lah port?

Could you get me a taxi, please?

Vous voulez m'appeler un taxi?

voo voolay mahplay uhn tahksee?

Is there any mail for me?

Y a-t-il du courrier pour moi?

ee yah teel dew kooryay poor mwah?

☞

Vous pouvez vous-même choisir votre emplacement.	You can pick your own site.
Votre emplacement vous sera attribué.	You'll be allocated a site.
Voici votre numéro d'emplacement.	This is your site number.
Vous devez coller ceci sur votre voiture.	Stick this on your car, please.
Ne perdez surtout pas cette carte.	Please don't lose this card.

7.2 Camping

Where's the manager?	Où est le gardien?
	oo eh luh gahrdyahn?
Are we allowed to camp here?	Pouvons-nous camper ici?
	poovawn noo kohnpay eesee?
There are...of us and...tents.	Nous sommes...personnes et nous avons...tentes.
	noo som...pehrson ay nooz ahvawn... tohnt
Can we pick our own place?	Pouvons-nous choisir nous-mêmes un emplacement?
	poovawn noo shwahzeer noo mehm uhn nohnplahsmohn?
Do you have a quiet spot for us?	Avez-vous un endroit calme pour nous?
	ahvay voo zuhn nohndrwah kahlm poor noo?
Do you have any other pitches available?	Vous n'avez pas d'autre emplacement libre?
	voo nahvay pah doatr ohnplahsmohn leebr?

Camping equipment

luggage space	l'espace (f.) bagages	*lehspahs bahgajh*
can opener	l'ouvre-boîte (m.)	*loovr bwaht*
butane gas bottle	la bouteille de butane	*lah bootehy duh bewtahnn*
pannier	la sacoche de vélo	*lah sahkosh duh vayloa*
gas cooker	le réchaud à gaz	*luh rayshoa ah gahz*
groundsheet	le tapis de sol	*luh tahpee duh sol*
mallet	le marteau	*luh mahrtoa*
hammock	le hamac	*luh ahmahk*
jerry can	le bidon d'essence	*luh beedawn dehssohns*
campfire	le feu de camp	*luh fuh duh kohn*
folding chair	la chaise pliante	*lah shehz plyohnt*
insulated picnic box	la glacière	*lah glahsyehr*
ice pack	le bac à glaçons	*luh bah kah glasawn*
compass	la boussole	*lah boosol*
wick	la mèche	*lah mehsh*
corkscrew	le tire-bouchon	*luh teer booshawn*
airbed	le matelas pneumatique	*luh mahtuhlah pnuhmahteek*
airbed plug	le bouchon du matelas pneumatique	*luh booshawn dew mahtuhlah pnemahteek*
pump	la pompe à air	*lah pawnp ah her*

It's too windy/sunny/ shady here.	Ici il y a trop de vent/soleil/ombre. *eesee eel ee yah troa duh vohn/sohlehy/awnbr*
It's too crowded here.	Il y a trop de monde ici. *eel ee yah troa duh mawnd eesee*

awning	l'auvent (m.)	*loavohn*
karimat	la natte	*lah naht*
pan	la casserole	*lah kahsrol*
pan handle	la poignée de casserole	*lah pwahnnyay duh kahsrol*
primus stove	le réchaud à pétrole	*luh rayshoa ah paytrol*
zip	la fermeture éclair	*lah fehrmuhtewr ayklehr*
backpack	le sac à dos	*luh sahk ah doa*
guy rope	la corde	*lah kord*
sleeping bag	le sac de couchage	*luh sahk duh kooshajh*
storm lantern	la lanterne-tempête	*lah lohntehrn-tohnpeht*
camp bed	le lit de camp	*luh lee duh kohn*
table	la table	*lah tahbl*
tent	la tente	*lah tohnt*
tent peg	le piquet	*luh peekeh*
tent pole	le mât	*luh mah*
vacuum flask	la bouteille thermos	*lah bootehy tehrmos*
water bottle	la gourde	*lah goord*
clothes peg	la pince à linge	*lah pahns ah lahnjh*
windbreak	le pare-vent	*luh pahrvohn*
torch	la torche électrique	*lah torsh aylehktreek*
pocket knife	le canif	*luh kahneef*

The ground's too hard/uneven.	Le sol est trop dur/irrégulier. *luh sohl eh troa dewr/eeraygewlyay*

Do you have a level spot for the camper/caravan/folding caravan?	Avez-vous un endroit plat pour le camping-car/la caravane/la caravane pliante?
	ahvay voo zuhn nohndrwah plah poor luh kohnpeeng kahr/lah kahrahvahnn/lah kahrahvahnn plyohnt?
Could we have adjoining pitches?	Pouvons-nous être l'un à côté de l'autre?
	poovawn noo zehtr luhn nah koatay duh loatr?
Can we park the car next to the tent?	La voiture, peut-elle être garée à côté de la tente?
	lah vwahtewr, puh tehl ehtr gahray ah koatay duh lah tohnt?
How much is it per person/tent/caravan/car?	Quel est le prix par personne/tente/caravane/voiture?
	kehl eh luh pree pahr pehrson/tohnt/kahrahvahnn/vwahtewr?
Are there any...?	Y a-t-il...?
	ee yah teel...?
– hot showers?	Y a-t-il des douches avec eau chaude?
	ee yah teel day doosh ahvehk oa shoad?
– washing machines?	Y a-t-il des machines à laver?
	ee yah teel day mahsheen ah lahvay?
Is there a...on the site?	Y a-t-il un...sur le terrain?
	ee ayh teel uhn...sewr luh tehrahn?
Is there a children's play area on the site?	Y a-t-il un terrain de jeux pour les enfants?
	ee yah teel uhn tehrahn duh jhuh poor lay zohnfohn?
Are there covered cooking facilities on the site?	Y a-t-il un endroit couvert pour cuisiner?
	ee yah teel uhn nohndrwa koovehr poor kweezeenay?
Are we allowed to barbecue here?	Pouvons-nous faire un barbecue?
	poovawn noo fehr uhn bahrbuhkew?
Are there any power points?	Y a-t-il des prises électriques?
	ee yah teel day preez aylehktreek?

s there drinking water?	Y a-t-il de l'eau potable?
	ee yah teel duh loa potabl?
Vhen's the rubbish collected?	Quand vide-t-on les poubelles?
	kohn veed-uh-tawn lay poobehl?
Do you sell gas bottles (butane gas/propane gas)?	Vendez-vous des bouteilles de gaz (butane/propane)?
	vohnday voo day bootehuhy duh gahz (bewtahnn/propahnn)?

7.3 Hotel/B&B/apartment/holiday house

Do you have a single/double room available?	Avez-vous une chambre libre pour une personne/deux personnes?
	ahvay voo zewn shohnbr leebr poor ewn pehrson/duh pehrson?
ber person/per room	par personne/par chambre
	pahr pehrson/pahr shohnbr
Does that include breakfast/ lunch/dinner?	Est-ce que le petit déjeuner/le déjeuner/ le dîner est compris?
	ehs kuh luh puhtee dayjhuhnay/luh dayjhuhnay/luh deenay eh kawnpree?
Could we have two adjoining rooms?	Pouvons-nous avoir deux chambres contiguës?
	poovawn noo zahvwahr duh shohnbr kawnteegew?
with/without toilet/ bath/shower	avec/sans toilettes/ salle de bains/douche
	ahvehk/sohn twahleht/sahl duh bahn/ doosh
(not) facing the street	(pas) du côté rue
	(pah) dew koatay rew
with/without a view of the sea	avec/sans vue sur la mer
	ahvehk/sohn vew sewr lah mehr
s there...in the hotel?	Y a-t-il...dans l'hôtel?
	ee yah teel...dohn loatehl?

Les toilettes et la douche sont au même étage/dans votre chambre.

You can find the toilet and shower on the same floor/en suite.

De ce côté, s'il vous plaît.

This way, please.

Votre chambre est au...étage, c'est le numéro...

Your room is on the... floor, number...

Is there a lift in the hotel?
Y a-t-il un ascenseur dans l'hôtel?
ee yah teel uhn nahsohnsuhr dohn loatehl?

Do you have room service?
Y a-t-il un service de chambre dans l'hôtel?
ee yah teel uhn sehrvees duh shohnbr dohn loatehl?

Could I see the room?
Puis-je voir la chambre?
pwee jhuh vwhar lah shohnbr?

I'll take this room.
Je prends cette chambre.
jhuh prohn seht shohnbr

We don't like this one.
Celle-ci ne nous plaît pas.
sehl see nuh noo pleh pah

Do you have a larger/ less expensive room?
Avez-vous une chambre plus grande/ moins chère?
avay voo zewn shohnbr plew grohnd/ mwahn shehr?

Could you put in a cot?
Pouvez-vous y ajouter un lit d'enfant?
poovay voo zee ahjhootay uhn lee dohnfohn?

What time's breakfast?
A quelle heure est le petit déjeuner?
ah kehl uhr eh luh puhtee dayjhuhnay?

Where's the dining room?
Où est la salle à manger?
oo eh lah sahl ah mohnjhay?

Can I have breakfast
in my room?

Puis-je prendre le petit déjeuner
dans la chambre?

*pwee jhuh prohndr luh puhtee
dayjhuhnay dohn lah shohnbr?*

Where's the emergency
exit/fire escape?

Où est la sortie de secours/l'escalier
de secours?

*oo eh lah sortee duh suhkoor/
lehskahlyay duh suhkoor?*

Where can I park my
car (safely)?

Où puis-je garer ma voiture (en sécurité)?

*oo pwee jhuh gahray mah vwahtewr
(ohn saykewreetay)?*

The key to room..., please.

La clef de la chambre..., s'il vous plaît.

lah klay duh lah shohnbr...,seel voo pleh

Could you put this in the safe,
please?

Puis-je mettre ceci dans votre
coffre-fort?

*pwee jhuh mehtr suhsee dohn votr
kofr for?*

Could you wake me at...
tomorrow?

Demain voulez-vous me réveiller à...
heures?

*duhmahn voolay voo muh rayvehyay ah...
uhr?*

Could you find a babysitter
for me?

Pouvez-vous m'aider à trouver une
baby-sitter?

*poovay voo mayday ah troovay ewn
behbee seetehr?*

Could I have an extra
blanket/pillow?

Puis-je avoir une couverture/oreiller
supplémentaire?

*pwee jhahvwahr ewn koovehrtewr/
ohrayay sewplaymohntehr?*

When are the sheets/towels/
tea towels changed?

Quand change-t-on les draps/les
serviettes-éponge/les torchons?

*kohn shohnjh tawn lay drah/lay sehrvyeht
aypawnjh/lay tohrshawn?*

7.4 Complaints

We can't sleep because it is too noisy.	Nous ne pouvons pas dormir à cause du bruit.
	noo nuh poovawn pah dormeer ah koaz dew brwee
Could you turn the radio down, please?	Est-ce que vous pouvez baisser un peu la radio?
	ehs kuh voo poovay behssay uhn puh lah rahdyoa?
We're out of toilet paper.	Il n'y a plus de papier hygiénique.
	eel nee yah plew duh pahpyay eejhyayneek
There aren't any.../ there's not enough...	Il n'y a pas de/pas assez de...
	eel nee yah pah duh/pah zahsay duh...
The bed linen's dirty.	La literie est sale.
	lah leetree eh sahl
The room hasn't been cleaned.	La chambre n'a pas été nettoyée.
	lah shohnbr nah pah zayatay nehtwahyay
The kitchen is not clean.	La cuisine n'est pas propre.
	lah kweezeen neh pah propr
The kitchen utensils are dirty.	Les ustensiles de cuisine sont sales.
	lay zewstohnseel duh kweezeen sawn sahl
The heater's not working.	Le chauffage ne marche pas.
	luh shoafajh nuh marsh pah
There's no (hot) water/electricity.	Il n'y a pas d'eau(chaude)/d'électricité.
	eel nee yah pah doa(shoad)/ daylehktreeseetay
...is broken	...est cassé
	...eh kahssay
Could you have that seen to?	Vous pouvez le faire réparer?
	voo poovay luh fehr raypahray?

Could I have another room/site?	Puis-je avoir une autre chambre/ un autre emplacement pour la tente?
	pwee jhuh ahvwahr ewn oatr shohnbr/ uhn noatr ohnplasmohn poor lah tohnt?
The bed creaks terribly.	Le lit grince énormément.
	luh lee grahns aynormaymohn
The bed sags.	Le lit s'affaisse.
	luh lee sahfehs
There are bugs/insects in our room.	Nous sommes incommodés par des bestioles/insectes.
	noo som zahnkomoday pahr day behstyol/day zahnsehkt
This place is full of mosquitos.	C'est plein de moustiques ici.
	seh plahn duh moosteek eesee
– cockroaches.	C'est plein de cafards.
	seh plahn duh kahfahr

7.5 Departure

See also **8.2 Settling the bill**

I'm leaving tomorrow. Could I settle my bill, please?	Je pars demain. Puis-je payer maintenant?
	jhuh pahr duhmahn. pwee jhuh payay mahntuhnohn?
What time should we check out?	A quelle heure devons-nous quitter la chambre?
	ah kehl uhr duhvawn noo keetay lah shohnbr?
Could I have my passport back, please?	Pouvez-vous me rendre mon passeport?
	poovay voo muh rohndr mawn pahspor?
We're in a terrible hurry.	Nous sommes très pressés.
	noo som treh prehssay

Could we leave our luggage here until we leave?

Nos valises peuvent rester ici jusqu'à notre départ?

noa vahleez puhv rehstay eesee jhewskah notr daypahr?

Thanks for your hospitality.

Merci pour votre hospitalité.

mehrsee poor votr ospeetahleetay

8. Money matters

● In general, banks are open 9–12 and 2–4pm; they are closed on Saturdays. In city centres they are often open at lunchtime. In tourist areas, the bank can be closed on Monday morning and open on Saturday morning. To exchange currency a proof of identity is usually required. The sign *Change* indicates that money can be exchanged.

8.1 Banks

Where can I find a cash point/ATM?	Où puis-je trouver un distributeur?
	oo peweejh troovay ahn deestreebewtuhr
Where can I find a bank/an exchange office around here?	Où puis-je trouver une banque/ un bureau de change par ici?
	oo pwee jhuh troovay ewn bohnk/uhn bewroa duh shohnjh pahr eesee?
Where can I cash this traveller's cheque?	Où puis-je encaisser ce chèque de voyage?
	oo pwee jhuh ohnkehssay suh shehk duh vwahyajh?
Can I cash this...here?	Puis-je encaisser ce...ici?
	pweejh ohnkehssay suh...eesee?
Can I withdraw money on my credit card here?	Puis-je retirer de l'argent avec une carte de crédit?
	pwee jhuh ruhteeray duh lahrjhohn ahvehk ewn kahrt duh kraydee?
What's the minimum/	Quel est le montant minimum/ maximum?
maximum amount?	*kehl eh luh mohntohn meeneemuhm/ mahxseemuhm?*
Can I take out less than that?	Puis-je retirer moins?
	pwee jhuh ruhteeray mwahn?
I've had some money transferred here. Has it arrived yet?	J'ai fait virer de l'argent par mandat télégraphique. Est-ce déjà arrivé?
	jhay feh veeray duh lahrjhohn pahr mohndah taylaygrahfeek. ehs dayjhah ahreevay?

Vous devez signer ici.	You have to sign here.
Vous devez remplir ceci.	You have to fill this out.
Puis-je voir votre passeport?	Could I see your passport?
Puis-je voir une pièce d'identité?	Could I see some identification?
Puis-je voir votre carte bancaire?	Could I see your bank card?

These are the details of my bank in the UK.
Voici les coordonnées de ma banque au Royaume-Uni.
vwahsee lay koa-ordonay duh mah bohnk oa rwahyoam ewnee

This is my bank account number.
Voici mon numéro de compte bancaire.
vwahsee mawn newmayroa duh kawnt bohnkehr

I'd like to change some money.
J'aimerais changer de l'argent.
jhehmuhreh shohnjhay duh lahrjhohn

– pounds into...
des livres sterling contre...
day leevr stehrleeng kawntr...

– dollars into...
des dollars contre...
day dolahr kawntr...

– euros into...
euros en
uhroh ahn

What's the exchange rate?
Le change est à combien?
luh shohnjh eh tah kawnbyahn?

Could you give me some small change with it?
Pouvez-vous me donner de la monnaie?
poovay voo muh donay duh lah moneh?

This is not right.
Ce n'est pas exact.
suh neh pah zehgzah

113

8.2 Settling the bill

Nous n'acceptons pas les cartes de crédit/les chèques de voyage/les devises étrangères.	Credit cards/traveller's cheques/ foreign currency are not accepted.

Could you put it on my bill?
Pouvez-vous le mettre sur mon compte?
poovay voo luh mehtr sewr mawn kawnt?

Does this amount include service?
Est-ce que le service est compris (dans la somme)?
ehs kuh luh sehrvees eh kawnpree (dohn lah som)?

Can I pay by...?
Puis-je payer avec...?
pwee jhuh payay ahvehk...?

Can I pay by credit card?
Puis-je payer avec une carte de crédit?
pwee jhuh payay ahvehk ewn kahrt duh kraydee?

Can I pay by traveller's cheque?
Puis-je payer avec un chèque de voyage?
pwee jhuh payay ahvehk uhn shehk duh vwahyajh?

Can I pay with foreign currency?
Puis-je vous payer en devises étrangères?
pwee jhuh voo payay ohn duhveez aytrohnjhehr?

You've given me too much/ you haven't given me enough change.
Vous m'avez trop/pas assez rendu.
voo mahvay troa/pah zahsay rohndew

Could you check this again, please?
Voulez-vous refaire le calcul?
voolay voo ruhfehr luh kahlkewl?

Could I have a receipt, please?

Pouvez-vous me donner un reçu/le ticket de caisse?

poovay voo muh donay uhn ruhsew/luh teekeh duh kehs?

I don't have enough money on me.

Je n'ai pas assez d'argent sur moi.

jhuh nay pah zahsay dahrjhohn sewr mwah

This is for you.

Voilà, c'est pour vous.

vwahlah seh poor voo

Keep the change.

Gardez la monnaie.

gahrday lah moneh

9. Communications

9.1 Post

● Post offices are open from Monday to Friday between 8am and 7pm.
In smaller towns the post office closes at lunch. On Saturday they are
open between 8am and 12 noon.
Stamps (*timbres*) are also available in a *tabac* (café that sells cigarettes
and matches).
The yellow letter box (*boîte aux lettres*) in the street and in the post office
has two rates: *tarif normal* (normal rate) and *tarif réduit* (reduced rate).
It is advisable to opt for the *tarif normal*.

colis	télégrammes
parcels	telegrams
mandats	**timbres**
money orders	stamps

Where's...?	Où est...?
	oo eh...?
Where's the post office?	Où est la poste?
	oo eh lah post?
Where's the main post office?	Où est la poste centrale?
	oo eh lah post sohntrahl?
Where's the postbox?	Où est la boîte aux lettres?
	oo eh lah bwaht oa lehtr?
Which counter should I go to...?	Quel est le guichet pour...?
	kehl eh luh gueesheh poor...?
– to send a fax?	Quel est le guichet pour les fax?
	kehl eh luh gueesheh poor lay fahx?
– to change money?	Quel est le guichet pour changer de l'argent?
	kehl eh luh gueesheh poor shohnjhay duh lahrjhohn?
Can I make photocopies/ send a fax here?	Puis-je faire des photocopies/envoyer un fax ici?
	pwee jhuh fehr day foatoakopee/ ohnvwahyay uhn fahx eesee?

Stamps

What's the postage for a...to...?	Combien faut-il sur une...pour...?
	kawnbyahn foa teel sewr ewn...poor...?
Are there enough stamps on it?	Y a-t-il suffisamment de timbres dessus?
	ee yah teel sewfeezahmohn duh tahnbr duhsew?
I'd like... ...euro stamps	Je voudrais...timbres à...
	jhuh voodreh...tahnbr ah...
I'd like to send this...	Je veux envoyer ce/cette...
	jhuh vuh zohnvwahyay suh/seht...
– express	Je veux envoyer ce/cette...en express.
	jhuh vuh zohnvwahyay suh/seht... ohn nehxprehs
– by air mail	Je veux envoyer ce/cette...par avion.
	jhuh vuh zohnvwahyay suh/seht... pahr ahvyawn
– by registered mail	Je veux envoyer ce/cette... en recommandé.
	jhuh vuh zohnvwahyay suh/seht... ohn ruhkomohnday

9.2 Telephone

See also **1.8 Telephone alphabet**

● All phone booths offer a direct international service to the UK or the US (00 + country code 44[UK] or 1[US]+ trunk code minus zero + number). Most phone booths will only accept phone cards (*télécartes*), which can be bought at the post office or in a *tabac*. Phone booths do not take incoming calls. Charges can no longer be reversed in France. A *carte globéo* (special card) can be obtained from any office of the telephone company, on presentation of a credit card and identification. Charges are then deducted from the bank account. When answering the phone in France, the person won't use his or her name, but will greet you with *allô* or *allô oui*?

Is there a phone box around here?	Y a-t-il une cabine téléphonique dans le coin?
	ee ah teel ewn kahbeen taylayfoneek dohn luh kwahn?
Could I use your phone, please?	Puis-je utiliser votre téléphone?
	pwee jhuh ewteeleezay votr taylayfon?
Do you have a (city/region)... phone directory?	Avez-vous un annuaire de la ville de.../ de la région de...?
	ahvay voo zuhn ahnnewehr duh lah veel duh.../duh lah rayjhyawn duh...?
Where can I get a phone card?	Où puis-je acheter une télécarte?
	oo pwee jhahshtay ewn taylaykahrt?
Could you give me...?	Pouvez-vous me donner...?
	poovay voo muh donay...?
– the number for international directory enquiries?	Pouvez-vous me donner le numéro des renseignements pour l'étranger?
	poovay voo muh donay luh newmayroa day rohnsehnyuhmohn poor laytrohnjhay?
– the number of room...?	Pouvez-vous me donner le numéro de la chambre...?
	poovay voo muh donay luh newmayroa duh lah shohnbr...?
– the international access code?	Pouvez-vous me donner le numéro international?
	poovay voo muh donay luh newmayroa ahntehrnahsyonahl?
– the country code for...?	Pouvez-vous me donner l'indicatif du pays pour...?
	poovay voo muh donay lahndeekahteef dew payee poor...?
– the trunk code for...?	Pouvez-vous me donner l'indicatif de...?
	poovay voo muh donay lahndeekahteef duh...?

– the number of...?	Pouvez-vous me donner le numéro d'abonné de...?
	poovay voo muh donay luh newmayroa dahbonay duh...?
Could you check if this number's correct?	Pouvez-vous vérifier si ce numéro est correct?
	poovay voo vayreefyay see suh newmayroa eh korehkt?
Can I dial international direct?	Puis-je téléphoner en automatique à l'étranger?
	pwee jhuh taylayfonay ohn noatoamahteek ah laytrohnjhay?
Do I have to go through the switchboard?	Dois-je appeler en passant par le standard?
	dwah jhahpuhlay ohn pahsohn pahr luh stohndahr?
Do I have to dial '0' first?	Dois-je d'abord faire le zéro?
	dwah jhuh dahbor fehr luh zayroa?
Do I have to book my calls?	Dois-je demander ma communication?
	dwah jhuh duhmohnday mah komewneekahsyawn?
Could you dial this number for me, please?	Voulez-vous m'appeler ce numéro?
	voolay voo mahpuhlay suh newmayroa?
Could you put me through to.../extension..., please?	Voulez-vous me passer.../le poste...?
	voolay voo muh pahsay.../luh post...?
What's the charge per minute?	Quel est le prix à la minute?
	kehl eh luh pree ah lah meenewt?
Have there been any calls for me?	Quelqu'un m'a-t-il appelé?
	kehlkuhn mah teel ahpuhlay?

The conversation

Hello, this is...	Allô, ici...
	ahloa, eesee...
Who is this, please?	Qui est à l'appareil?
	kee eh tah lahpahrehy?

Is this...?	Je parle à...?
	jhuh pahrl ah...?
I'm sorry, I've dialled the wrong number.	Pardon, je me suis trompé(e) de numéro.
	pahrdawn, jhuh muh swee trawnpay duh newmayroa
I can't hear you.	Je ne vous entends pas.
	jhuh nuh voo zohntohn pah
I'd like to speak to...	Je voudrais parler à...
	jhuh voodreh pahrlay ah...
Is there anybody who speaks English?	Y a-t-il quelqu'un qui parle l'anglais?
	ee yah teel kehlkuhn kee pahrl lohngleh?
Extension... please.	Pouvez-vous me passer le poste...?
	poovay voo muh pahsay luh post...?
Could you ask him/her to call me back?	Voulez-vous demander qu'il/qu'elle me rappelle?
	voolay voo duhmohnday keel/kehl muh rahpehl?

👉

On vous demande au téléphone.	There's a phone call for you.
Vous devez d'abord faire le zéro.	You have to dial '0' first.
Vous avez un instant?	One moment, please.
Je n'obtiens pas de réponse.	There's no answer.
La ligne est occupée.	The line's engaged.
Vous voulez attendre?	Could you hold?
Je vous passe la communication.	Putting you through.
Vous vous êtes trompé de numéro.	You've got the wrong number.
Il/elle n'est pas ici en ce moment.	He's/she's not here right now.
Vous pouvez le/la rappeler à...	He'll/she'll be back...
C'est le répondeur automatique de...	This is the answering machine of...

My name's... My number's...	Mon nom est...Mon numéro est...
	mawn nawn eh...mawn newmayroa eh...
Could you tell him/her I called?	Voulez-vous dire que j'ai appelé?
	voolay voo deer kuh jhay ahpuhlay?
I'll call back tomorrow.	Je rappellerai demain.
	jhuh rahpehluhray duhmah

9.3 Email and internet

Can I use the internet/check my emails here?	Est-ce que je peux utiliser Internet / consulter mes emails ici?
	ehs kuh juh puh ewteeleezay ahntehrneht/kawnsewltay may zeemehyl eesee?
Do you have (free) WiFi?	Est-ce que vous avez le Wifi (gratuit)?
	ehs kuh voo ahvay luh weefee (grahtewee)?
Where can I find an internet café?	Où est-ce que je peux trouver un café internet?
	oo ehs kuh juh puh troovay ahn kahfay ahntehrneht?
How much does the internet cost per hour?	Combien coûte la connexion par heure ?
	kawnbyahn koot lah konehksyawn ahntehrneht pahr uhr?
Can I connect my computer/laptop here?	Est-ce que je peux connecter mon ordinateur/ordinateur portable ici?
	ehs kuh juh puh konehktay mawn ohrdeenahtuhr eesee?
What is the password?	Quel est le mot de passe?
	kehl ay luh moh duh pass?
Can I use a printer?	Est-ce que je peux utiliser l'imprimante?
	ehs kuh juh puh ewteeleezay lahnpreemohnt?

Are you on Facebook?	Avez-vous Facebook? [formal]
	ahvay voo Facebook?
	Est-ce que tu as Facebook? [informal]
	ehs kuh tew ah Facebook?
Can I add you as a friend?	Est-ce que je peux vous ajouter en ami sur Facebook? [formal]
	ehs kuh juh puh voo zahjootay ohn ahmee sewr Facebook?
	Est-ce que je peux t'ajouter sur Facebook? [informal]
	ehs kuh juh puh tahjootay sewr Facebook?
Are you on Twitter?	Etes-vous sur Twitter? [formal]
	eht voo sewr Twitter?
	Est-ce que tu es sur Twitter? [informal]
	ehs kuh tew ay sewr Twitter?
What is your username?	Quel est votre nom d'utilisateur? [formal]
	kehl ay vohtr nawn dewteeleezahtuhr?
	Quel est ton nom d'utilisateur? [informal]
	kehl ay tawn nawn dewteeleezahtuhr?
My email address is...	Mon adresse email est...
	mawn ahdrehs eemayl ay...
What is your email address?	Quelle est votre/ton adresse email?
	kehl ay vohtr/tawn ahdrehs eemayl?

10. Shopping

Opening times: Tuesday to Saturday 8/9am–1pm and 2.30–7pm.
On Mondays shops are closed in the morning or for the entire day. On
Sunday mornings grocers and bakers are usually open, and markets are
open until 1pm. Supermarkets and department stores in nearly all cities
are open until 8pm once a week. Chemists display the list of *pharmacies
e garde* (those open on Sundays and after hours), but you may be
charged double in some cities. You may be asked to pay in advance for
shoe repairs and dry cleaning.

10.1 Shopping conversations

Where can I get...?	Dans quel magasin puis-je acheter...?
	dohn kehl mahgahzahn pwee jhahshtay...?
When does this shop open?	A quelle heure ouvre ce magasin?
	ah kehl uhr oovr suh mahgahzahn?
Could you tell me where the...department is?	Pouvez-vous m'indiquer le rayon de...?
	poovay voo mahndeekay luh rayawn duh...?
Could you help me, please? I'm looking for...	Pouvez-vous m'aider? Je cherche...
	poovay voo mayday? jhuh shehrsh...
Do you sell English/ American newspapers?	Vendez-vous des journaux anglais/ américains?
	vohnday voo day jhoornoa ohngleh/ ahmayreekahn?
No, I'd like...	Non. J'aimerais...
	nawn. jhehmuhreh...
I'm just looking, if that's all right.	Je jette un coup d'oeil, si c'est permis.
	jhuh jheht uhn koo duhy, see seh pehrmee

On s'occupe de vous?	Are you being served?
Vous désirez autre chose?	Anything else?

antiquités
antiques
appareils électriques
electrical appliances
bijoutier
jeweller
blanchisserie
laundry
boucherie
butcher
boulangerie
bakery
centre commercial
shopping centre
charcuterie
delicatessen
coiffeur (femmes/
  hommes)
hairdresser
  (women/men)
cordonnier
cobbler
crémerie
dairy
épicerie
grocery store
fleuriste
florist
fruits et légumes
greengrocer
galerie marchande
shopping arcade

grand magasin
department store
laverie automatique
launderette
librairie
bookshop
magasin
shop
magasin
  d'ameublement
furniture shop
magasin d'appareils
  photographiques
camera shop
magasin de
  bicyclettes
bicycle shop
magasin de
  bricolage
DIY-store
magasin de jouets
toy shop
magasin de disques
music shop
magasin de
  souvenirs
souvenir shop
magasin de sport
sports shop
magasin de vins et
  spiritueux
off-licence

magasin diététique
health food shop
marché
market
marché aux puces
fleamarket
mercerie
draper
pâtisserie
cake shop
pharmacie
chemist
poissonnerie
fishmonger
produits ménagers/
  droguerie
household goods
quincaillerie
hardware shop
réparateur de
  bicyclettes
bicycle repairs
salon de beauté
beauty parlour
salon de dégustation
  de glaces
ice-cream parlour
supermarché
supermarket
tabac
tobacconist
teinturerie
dry-cleaner

Yes, I'd also like…   Oui, donnez-moi aussi…
                            wee, donay mwah oasee…

No, thank you. That's all.	Non, je vous remercie. Ce sera tout.
	nawn, jhuh voo ruhmehrsee.
	suh suhrah too
Could you show me...?	Pouvez-vous me montrer...?
	poovay voo muh mawntray...?
I'd prefer...	Je préfère... *jhuh prayfehr...*
This is not what	Ce n'est pas ce que je cherche.
I'm looking for.	*suh neh pah suh kuh jhuh shehrsh*
Thank you. I'll keep looking.	Merci. Je chercherai ailleurs.
	mehrsee. jhuh shehrshuhray ahyuhr
Do you have something...?	Vous n'avez pas quelque chose de...?
	voo nahvay pah kehlkuh shoaz duh...?
- less expensive?	Vous n'avez pas quelque chose
	de moins cher?
	voo nahvay pah kehlkuh shoaz duh
	mwahn shehr?
- something smaller?	Vous n'avez pas quelque chose
	de plus petit?
	voo nahvay pah kehlkuh shoaz
	duh plew puhtee?
- something larger?	Vous n'avez pas quelque chose
	de plus grand?
	voo nahvay pah kehlkuh shoaz
	duh plew grohn?
I'll take this one.	Je prends celui-ci.
	jhuh prohn suhlwee see
Does it come	Y a-t-il un mode d'emploi avec?
with instructions?	*ee yah teel uhn mod dohnplwah ahvehk?*
It's too expensive.	Je le trouve trop cher.
	jhuh luh troov troa shehr
I'll give you...	Je vous offre... *jhuh voo zofr...*
Could you keep this for me?	Voulez-vous me le mettre de côté?
I'll come back for it later.	Je reviendrai le chercher tout à l'heure.
	voolay voo muh luh mehtr duh koatay?
	jhuh ruhvyahndray luh shehrshay too
	tah luhr

Je suis désolé, nous n'en avons pas.	I'm sorry, we don't have that.
Je suis désolé, le stock est épuisé.	I'm sorry, we're sold out.
Je suis désolé, ce ne sera pas livré avant...	I'm sorry, that won't be in until...
Vous pouvez payer à la caisse.	You can pay at the cash desk.
Nous n'acceptons pas les cartes de crédit.	We don't accept credit cards.
Nous n'acceptons pas les chèques de voyage.	We don't accept traveller's cheques.
Nous n'acceptons pas les devises étrangères.	We don't accept foreign currency.

Have you got a bag for me, please?	Vous avez un sac?
	voo zahvay uhn sahk?
Could you giftwrap it, please?	Vous pouvez l'emballer dans un papier cadeau?
	voo poovay lohnbahlay dohn zuhn pahpyay kahdoa?

10.2 Food

I'd like a hundred grams of..., please	Je voudrais cent grammes de...
	jhuh voodreh sohn grahm duh...
– five hundred grams/half a kilo of...	Je voudrais une livre de...
	jhuh voodreh zewn leevr duh...
– a kilo of...	Je voudrais un kilo de...
	jhuh voodreh zuhn keeloa duh...
Could you...it for me, please?	Vous voulez me le...?
	voo voolay muh luh...?

Could you slice it/dice it for me, please?

Vous voulez me le couper en tranches/morceaux?

voo voolay muh luh koopay ohn trohnsh/mohrsoa?

Could you grate it for me, please?

Vous voulez me le râper?

voo voolay muh luh rahpay?

Can I order it?

Puis-je le commander?

pwee jhuh luh komohnday?

I'll pick it up tomorrow/at...

Je viendrai le chercher demain/à... heures.

jhuh vyahndray luh shehrshay duhmahn/ ah...uhr

Can you eat/drink this?

Est-ce mangeable/buvable?

ehs mohnjhahbl/bewvahbl?

What's in it?

Qu'y a-t-il dedans?

kee yah teel duhdohn?

10.3 Clothing and shoes

I saw something in the window. Shall I point it out?

J'ai vu quelque chose dans la vitrine. Je vous le montre?

jhay vew kehlkuh shoaz dohn lah veetreen. jhuh voo lah mawntr?

I'd like something to go with this.

J'aimerais quelque chose pour aller avec ceci.

jhehmuhreh kehlkuh shoaz poor ahlay ahvehk suhsee

Do you have shoes to match this?

Avez-vous des chaussures de la même couleur que ça?

ahvay voo day shoasewr duh lah mehm kooluhr kuh sah?

I'm a size...in the UK.

Je fais du...au Royaume-Uni.

jhuh feh dew...oa rwahyoam ewnee

Can I try this on?

Puis-je l'essayer?

pwee jhuh lehsayay?

Ne pas repasser	**Nettoyage à sec**	**Étendre humide**
Do not iron	Dry clean	Drip dry
Laver à la main	**Ne pas essorer**	**Laver à la machine**
Hand wash	Do not spin dry	Machine wash

Where's the fitting room?	Où est la cabine d'essayage?
	oo eh lah kahbeen dehsayahjh?
It doesn't fit.	Cela ne me va pas.
	suhlah nuh muh vah pah
This is the right size.	C'est la bonne taille.
	seh lah bon tahy
It doesn't suit me.	Cela ne me convient pas.
	suhlah nuh muh kawnvyahn pah
Do you have this in...?	L'avez-vous aussi en...?
	lahvay voo zoasee ohn...?
The heel's too high/low.	Je trouve le talon trop haut/bas.
	jhuh troov luh tahlawn troa oa/bah
Is this/are these genuine leather?	Est-ce/sont-elles en cuir?
	eh suh/sawn tehl ohn kweer?
I'm looking for a...for a...-year-old baby/child.	Je cherche un...pour un bébé/enfant de...ans.
	jhuh shehrsh uhn...poor uhn baybay/ohnhfohn duh...ohn
I'd like a... ...	J'aurais aimé un...de...
	jhoareh zaymay uhn... duh...
– silk	J'aurais aimé un...de soie.
	jhoareh zaymay uhn...duh swah
– cotton	J'aurais aimé un...de coton.
	jhoareh zaymay uhn...duh koatawn
– woollen	J'aurais aimé un...de laine.
	jhoareh zaymay uhn...duh lehn
– linen	J'aurais aimé un...de lin.
	jhoareh zaymay uhn...duh lahn
What temperature can I wash it at?	A quelle température puis-je le laver?
	ah kehl tohnpayrahtewr pwee jhuh luh lahvay?

Will it shrink in the wash?   Cela rétrécit au lavage?
suhlah raytraysee oa lahvahjh?

At the cobbler

Could you mend these shoes?   Pouvez-vous réparer ces chaussures?
poovay voo raypahray say shoasewr?

Could you put new soles/
heels on these?   Pouvez-vous y mettre de nouvelles
semelles/nouveaux talons?
*poovay voo zee mehtr duh noovehl
suhmehl/noovoa tahlawn?*

When will they be ready?   Quand seront-elles prêtes?
kohn suhrawn tehl preht?

I'd like..., please   Je voudrais...
jhuh voodreh...

- a tin of shoe polish   Je voudrais une boîte de cirage.
jhuh voodreh zewn bwaht duh seerahjh

- a pair of shoelaces   Je voudrais une paire de lacets.
jhuh voodreh zewn pehr duh lahseh

10.4 Photographs: digital and film

I need a memory card/
charger/battery for
my digital camera.   J'ai besoin d'une carte mémoire/
d'un chargeur de batterie/de piles
pour mon appareil photo numérique.
*jay buhzwahn dewn kahrt maymwahr/
dahn shahrjuhr duh bahtuhree/duh
peel poor mawn ahpahrehy fohtoh
newmeyreek*

Can I print digital photos here?   Est-ce que je peux imprimer des photos
numériques ici?
*ehs kuh juh puh ahnpreemay day fohtoh
newmeyreek eesee?*

How much does it
cost per image?   Quel est le prix par image?
kehl ay luh pree pahr eemahjh?

What sizes are available?	Quelles sont les tailles disponibles?
	kehl sawn lay tahy deespohneebl?
Can you put my photos on a CD?	Est-ce que vous pouvez mettre mes photos sur un CD?
	ehs kuh voo poovay mehtr may fohtoh sewr ahn sayday?
I'd like a film for this camera, please.	Je voudrais un rouleau de pellicules pour cet appareil.
	jhuh voodreh zuhn rooloa duh payleekewl poor seht ahpahrehy
Where can I have a passport photo taken?	Où puis-je faire faire une photo d'identité?
	oo pwee jhuh fehr fehr ewn foatoa deedohnteetay?

Processing and prints

I'd like to have this film developed/printed, please.	Je voudrais faire développer/tirer ce film.
	jhuh voodreh fehr dayvuhlopay/teeray suh feelm
I'd like...prints from each negative.	Je voudrais...tirages de chaque négatif.
	jhuh voodreh...teerahjh duh shahk naygahteef
glossy/matte	brillant/mat	*breeyohn/maht*
6x9	six sur neuf	*sees sewr nuhf*
I'd like to re-order these photos.	Je veux faire refaire cette photo.
	jhuh vuh fehr ruhfehr seht foatoa
I'd like to have this photo enlarged.	Je veux faire agrandir cette photo.
	jhuh vuh fehr ahgrohndeer seht foatoa
How much is processing?	Combien coûte le développement?
	kawnbyahn koot luh dayvuhlopmohn?
How much is printing?	Combien coûte le tirage?
	kawnbyahn koot luh teerahjh?
– to re-order	Combien coûte la commande supplémentaire?
	kawnbyahn koot lah komohnd sewplaymohntehr?

the enlargement	Combien coûte l'agrandissement?
	kawnbyahn koot lahgrohndeesmohn?
When will they be ready?	Quand seront-elles prêtes?
	kohn suhrawn tehl preht?

10.5 At the hairdresser's

Do I have to make an appointment?	Dois-je prendre un rendez-vous?
	dwah jhuh prohndr uhn rohnday voo?
Can I come in straight away?	Pouvez-vous vous occuper de moi immédiatement?
	poovay voo voo zokewpay duh mwah eemaydyahtmohn?
How long will I have to wait?	Combien de temps dois-je attendre?
	kawnbyahn duh tohn dwah jhahtohndr?
I'd like a shampoo/haircut.	Je veux me faire laver/couper les cheveux.
	jhuh vuh muh fehr lahvay/koopay lay shuhvuh
Do you have a colour chart, please?	Avez-vous une carte de coloration s'il vous plaît?
	ahvay voo zewn kahrt duh kolorahsyawn seel voo pleh?
I want to keep it the same colour.	Je veux garder la même couleur.
	jhuh vuh gahrday lah mehm kooluhr
I'd like it darker/lighter.	Je les veux plus sombres/clairs.
	jhuh lay vuh plew sawmbr/klehr
I'd like/I don't want hairspray.	Je veux de la/ne veux pas de laque.
	jhuh vuh duh la/nuh vuh pah duh lahk
- gel.	Je veux du/ne veux pas de gel.
	jhuh vuh dew/ nuh vuh pah duh jhehl
- lotion.	Je veux de la/ne veux pas de lotion.
	jhuh vuh duh lah/nuh vuh pah duh loasyawn

Quelle coupe de cheveux désirez-vous?	How do you want it cut?
Quelle coiffure désirez-vous?	What style did you have in mind?
Quelle couleur désirez-vous?	What colour do you want it?
Est-ce la bonne température?	Is the temperature all right for you?
Voulez-vous lire quelque chose?	Would you like something to read?
Voulez-vous boire quelque chose?	Would you like a drink?
C'est ce que vous vouliez?	Is this what you had in mind?

I'd like a short fringe.
Je veux ma frange courte.
jhuh vuh mah frohnjh koort

Not too short at the back.
Je ne veux pas la nuque trop courte.
jhuh nuh vuh pah lah newk troa koort

Not too long here.
Ici je ne les veux pas trop longs.
eesee jhuh nuh lay vuh pah troa lawn

I'd like a facial.
J'aimerais un masque de beauté.
jhehmuhreh zuhn mahsk duh boatay

– a manicure.
J'aimerais qu'on me fasse les ongles.
jhehmuhreh kawn muh fahs lay zawngl

– a massage.
J'aimerais un massage.
jhehmuhreh zuhn mahsahjh

Could you trim my fringe?
Pouvez-vous égaliser ma frange?
poovay voo zaygahleezay mah frohnjh?

– my beard?
Pouvez-vous égaliser ma barbe?
poovay voo zaygahleezay mah bahrb?

– my moustache?
Pouvez-vous égaliser ma moustache?
poovay voo zaygahleezay mah moostahsh?

I'd like a shave, please.
Pouvez-vous me raser s'il vous plaît?
poovay voo muh rahzay seel voo pleh?

I'd like a wet shave, please.
Je veux être rasé au rasoir à main.
jhuh vuh zehtr rahzay oa rahzwahr ah mahn

11. At the Tourist Information Centre

11.1 Places of interest

Where's the Tourist Information, please?	Où est l'office de tourisme?
	oo eh lofees duh tooreesm?
Do you have a city map?	Avez-vous un plan de la ville?
	ahvay voo zuhn plohn duh lah veel?
Where is the museum?	Où est le musée?
	oo eh luh mewzay?
Where can I find a church?	Où puis-je trouver une église?
	oo pwee jhuh troovay ewn aygleez?
Could you give me some information about...?	Pouvez-vous me renseigner sur...?
	poovay voo muh rohnsehnyay sewr...?
How much is that?	Combien ça coûte?
	kawnbyahn sah koot?
What are the main places of interest?	Quelles sont les curiosités les plus importantes?
	kehl sawn lay kewryoseetay lay plewz ahnportohnt?
Could you point them out on the map?	Pouvez-vous les indiquer sur la carte?
	poovay voo lay zahndeekay sewr lah kahrt?
What do you recommend?	Que nous conseillez-vous?
	kuh noo kawnsehyay voo?
We'll be here for a few hours.	Nous restons ici quelques heures.
	noo rehstawn zeesee kehlkuh zuhr
– a day.	Nous restons ici une journée.
	noo rehstawn zeesee ewn jhoornay
– a week.	Nous restons ici une semaine.
	noo rehstawn zeesee ewn suhmehn
We're interested in...	Nous sommes intéressés par...
	noo som zahntayrehsay pahr...
Is there a scenic walk around the city?	Pouvons-nous faire une promenade en ville?
	poovawn noo fehr ewn promuhnahd ohn veel?
How long does it take?	Combien de temps dure-t-elle?
	kawnbyahn duh tohn dewr tehl?

Where does it start/end?	Où est le point de départ/d'arrivée?	
	oo eh luh pwahn duh daypahr/ dahreevay?	
Are there any boat cruises here?	Y a-t-il des bateaux-mouches?	
	ee yah teel day bahtoa moosh?	
Where can we board?	Où pouvons-nous embarquer?	
	oo poovawn noo zohnbahrkay?	
Are there any bus tours?	Y a-t-il des promenades en bus?	
	ee yah teel day promuhnahd ohn bews?	
Where do we get on?	Où devons-nous monter?	
	oo devawn noo mawntay?	
Is there a guide who speaks English?	Y a-t-il un guide qui parle l'anglais?	
	ee yah teel uhn gueed kee pahrl lohngleh?	
What trips can we take around the area?	Quelles promenades peut-on faire dans la région?	
	kehl promuhnahd puh tawn fehr dohn lah rayjhyawn?	
Are there any excursions?	Y a-t-il des excursions?	
	ee yah teel day zehxkewrsyawn?	
Where do they go to?	Où vont-elles?	
	oo vawn tehl?	
We'd like to go to...	Nous voulons aller à...	
	noo voolawn zahlay ah...	
How long is the trip?	Combien de temps dure l'excursion?	
	kawnbyahn duh tohn dewr lehxkewrsyawn?	
How long do we stay in...?	Combien de temps restons-nous à...?	
	kawnbyahn duh tohn rehstawn noo zah...?	
Are there any guided tours?	Y a-t-il des visites guidées?	
	ee yah teel day veezeet gueeday?	
How much free time will we have there?	Combien de temps avons-nous de libre?	
	kawnbyahn duh tohn ahvawn noo duh leebr?	
We want to go hiking.	Nous voulons faire une randonnée.	
	noo voolawn fehr ewn rohndonay	
Can we hire a guide?	Pouvons-nous prendre un guide?	
	poovawn noo prohndr uhn gueed?	

What time does...open/close?	A quelle heure ouvre/ferme...?
	ah kehl uhr oovr/fehrm...?
What days is...open/closed?	Quels sont les jours d'ouverture/ de fermeture de...?
	kehl sawn lay jhoor doovehrtewr/ duh fehrmuhtewr duh...?
What's the admission price?	Quel est le prix d'entrée?
	kehl eh luh pree dohntray?
Is there a group discount?	Y a-t-il une réduction pour les groupes?
	ee yah teel ewn raydewksyawn poor lay groop?
Is there a child discount?	Y a-t-il une réduction pour les enfants?
	ee yah teel ewn raydewksyawn poor lay zohnfohn?
Is there a student discount?	Est-ce qu'il y a une réduction pour les étudiants?
	ehs keel ee ah ewn raydewkseeawn poor lay aytewdeeohn?
Is there a discount for pensioners?	Y a-t-il une réduction pour les personnes de plus de soixante-cinq ans?
	ee yah teel ewn raydewksyawn poor lay pehrson duh plew duh swahssohnt sahnk ohn?
Can I take (flash) photos/can I film here?	M'est-il permis de prendre des photos(avec flash)/filmer ici?
	meh teel pehrmee duh prohndr day foatoa(ahvehk flahsh)/feelmay eesee?
Do you have any postcards of...?	Vendez-vous des cartes postales de...?
	vohnday voo day kahrt postahl duh...?
Do you have an English...?	Avez-vous un...en anglais?
	ahvay voo zuhn...ohn nohngleh?
– an English catalogue?	Avez-vous un catalogue en anglais?
	ahvay voo zuhn kahtahlog ohn nohngleh?
– an English programme?	Avez-vous un programme en anglais?
	ahvay voo zuhn prograhm ohn nohngleh?

- an English brochure?

Avez-vous une brochure en anglais?
ahvay voo zewn broshewr ohn nohngleh?

11.2 Going out

● In French theatres you are usually shown to your seat by an usherette from whom you can buy a programme. It is customary to tip. At the cinema most films are dubbed (*version française*). In large cities subtitled versions are often screened, advertised as *version originale* or *V.O.* If the publicity does not mention *V.O.*, the film will be dubbed. *L'Officiel des spectacles* (an entertainment guide) can be obtained from newspaper kiosks.

Do you have this
week's/month's
entertainment guide?

Avez-vous le journal des spectacles
de cette semaine/de ce mois?
*ahvay voo luh jhoornal day spehktahkl
duh seht suhmehn/duh suh mwah?*

What's on tonight?

Que peut-on faire ce soir?
kuh puh tawn fehr suh swahr?

We want to go to...

Nous voulons aller au...
noo voolawn zahlay oa...

Which films are showing?

Quels films passe-t-on?
kehl feelm pah stawn?

What sort of film is that?

Qu'est-ce que c'est comme film?
kehs kuh seh kom feelm?

suitable for all ages

pour tous les âges
poor too lay zahjh

not suitable for children
under 12/16 years

pour les plus de douze ans/seize ans
poor lay plew duh dooz ohn/sehz ohn

original version

version originale
vehrsyawn oreejheenahl

subtitled

sous-titré
soo teetray

dubbed

doublé
dooblay

What's on at...?	Qu'y a-t-il au...?
	kee yah teel oa...?
– the theatre?	Qu'y a-t-il au théâtre?
	kee yah teel oa tayahtr?
– the concert hall?	Qu'y a-t-il à la salle des concerts?
	kee yah teel ah lah sahl day kawnsehr?
– the opera?	Qu'y a-t-il à l'opéra?
	kee yah teel ah loapayrah?
Where can I find a good nightclub around here?	Où se trouve une bonne boîte de nuit par ici?
	oo suh troov ewn bon bwaht duh nwee pahr eesee?
Is it members only?	Exige-t-on une carte de membre?
	ehgzeejh-tawn ewn kahrt duh mohnbr?
Is it evening wear only?	La tenue de soirée, est-elle obligatoire?
	lah tuhnew duh swahray, eh tehl obleegahtwahr?
Should I/we dress up?	La tenue de soirée, est-elle souhaitée?
	lah tuhnew duh swahray ehtehl sooehtay?
What time does the show start?	A quelle heure commence la représentation?
	ah kehl uhr komohns lah ruhprayzohntahsyawn?
When's the next football match?	Quand est le prochain match de football?
	kohn teh luh proshahn mahtch duh footbohl?
Who's playing?	Qui joue contre qui?
	kee jhoo kawntr kee?

11.3 Booking tickets

Could you book some tickets for us?
Pouvez-vous nous faire une réservation?
poovay voo noo fehr ewn rayzehrvahsyawn?

We'd like to book... seats/a table...
Nous voulons...places/une table...
noo voolawn...plahs/ewn tahbl...

– in the stalls.
Nous voulons...places à l'orchestre.
noo voolawn...plahs ah lorkehstr

– on the balcony.
Nous voulons...places au balcon.
noo voolawn...plahs oa bahlkawn

– box seats.
Nous voulons...places dans les loges.
noo voolawn...plahs dohn lay lojh

– a table at the front.
Nous voulons...une table à l'avant.
noo voolawn...ewn tahbl ah lahvohn

– in the middle.
Nous voulons...places au milieu.
noo voolawn...plahs oa meelyuh

– at the back.
Nous voulons...places à l'arrière.
noo voolawn...plahs ah lahryehr

Could I book...seats for the...o'clock performance?
Puis-je réserver...places pour la représentation de...heures?
pwee jhuh rayzehrvay...plahs poor lah ruhprayzohntahsyawn duh...uhr?

Are there any seats left for tonight?
Reste-t-il encore des places pour ce soir?
rehst-uh-teel ohnkor day plahs poor suh swahr?

How much is a ticket?
Combien coûte un billet?
kawnbyahn koot uhn beeyeh?

When can I pick the tickets up?
Quand puis-je venir chercher les billets?
kohn pwee jhuh vuhneer shehrshay lay beeyeh?

I've got a reservation.
J'ai réservé.
jhay rayzehrvay

My name's...
Mon nom est...
mawn nawn eh...

Vous voulez réserver pour quelle représentation?	Which performance do you want to book for?
Où voulez-vous vous asseoir?	Where would you like to sit?
Tout est vendu.	Everything's sold out.
Il ne reste que des places debout.	We've only got standing spaces left.
Il ne reste que des places au balcon.	We've only got balcony seats left.
Il ne reste que des places au poulailler.	We've only got seats left in the gallery.
Il ne reste que des places d'orchestre.	We've only got stalls seats left.
Il ne reste que des places à l'avant.	We've only got seats left at the front.
Il ne reste que des places à l'arrière.	We've only got seats left at the back.
Combien de places voulez-vous?	How many seats would you like?
Vous devez venir chercher les billets avant...heures.	You'll have to pick up the tickets before...o'clock.
Puis-je voir vos billets?	Tickets, please.
Voici votre place.	This is your seat.
Vous n'êtes pas aux bonnes places.	You're in the wrong seats.

12. Sports

12.1 Sporting questions

Where can we...around here?	Où pouvons-nous...?
	oo poovawn noo...?
Is there a...around here?	Y a-t-il un...dans les environs?
	ee yah teel uhn...dohn lay zohnveerawn?
Can I hire a...here?	Puis-je louer un...ici?
	pwee jhuh looay uhn...eesee?
Can I take...lessons?	Puis-je prendre des cours de...?
	pwee jhuh prohndr day koor duh...?
How much is that per hour/ per day/a turn?	Quel est le prix à l'heure/ à la journée/à chaque fois?
	kehl eh luh pree ah luhr/ah lah jhoornay/ ah shahk fwah?
Do I need a permit for that?	A-t-on besoin d'un permis?
	ah tawn buhzwahn duhn pehrmee?
Where can I get the permit?	Où puis-je obtenir le permis?
	oo pwee jhuh obtuhneer luh pehrmee?

12.2 By the waterfront

Is it a long way to the sea still?	La mer, est-elle encore loin?
	lah mehr eh tehl ohnkor lwahn?
Is there a...around here?	Y a-t-il un...dans les environs?
	ee yah teel uhn...dohn lay zohnveerawn?
– a public swimming pool?	Y a-t-il une piscine dans les environs?
	ee yah teel ewn peeseen dohn lay zohnveerawn?
– a sandy beach?	Y a-t-il une plage de sable dans les environs?
	ee yah teel ewn plahjh duh sahbl dohn lay zohnveerawn?

– a nudist beach?	Y a-t-il une plage pour nudistes dans les environs?
	ee yah teel ewn plahjh poor newdeest dohn lay zohnveerawn?
– mooring?	Y a-t-il un embarcadère pour les bateaux dans les environs?
	ee yah teel uhn nohnbahrkahdehr poor lay bahtoa dohn lay zohnveerawn?
Are there any rocks here?	Y a-t-il aussi des rochers ici?
	ee yah teel oasee day roshay eesee?
When's high/low tide?	Quand est la marée haute/basse?
	kohn teh lah mahray oat/bahs?
What's the water temperature?	Quelle est la température de l'eau?
	kehl eh lah tohnpayratewr duh loa?
Is it (very) deep here?	Est-ce (très) profond ici?
	ehs (treh) proafawn eesee?
Can you stand here?	A-t-on pied ici?
	ah tawn pyay eesee?
Is it safe to swim here?	Peut-on nager en sécurité ici?
	puh tawn nahjhay ohn saykewreetay eesee?
Are there any currents?	Y a-t-il des courants?
	ee yah teel day koorohn?
Are there any rapids/ waterfalls in this river?	Est-ce que cette rivière a des courants rapides/des chutes d'eau?
	ehs kuh seht reevyehr ah day koorohn rahpeed/day shewt doa?

Danger	**Pêche interdite**	**Baignade interdite**
Danger	No fishing	No swimming
Pêche	**Surf interdit**	**Seulement avec permis**
Fishing water	No surfing	Permits only

What does that flag/buoy mean?	Que signifie ce drapeau/cette bouée là-bas?
	kuh seenyeefee suh drahpoa/seht booway lah bah?
Is there a life-guard on duty here?	Y a-t-il un maître nageur qui surveille?
	ee yah teel uhn mehtr nahjhuhr kee sewrvehy?
Are dogs allowed here?	Les chiens sont admis ici?
	lay shyahn sawn tahdmee eesee?
Is camping on the beach allowed?	Peut-on camper sur la plage?
	puh tawn kohnpay sewr lah plahjh?
Are we allowed to build a fire here?	Peut-on faire un feu ici?
	puh tawn fehr uhn fuh eesee?

12.3 In the snow

Can I take ski lessons here?	Puis-je prendre des leçons de ski?
	pwee jhuh prohndr day luhsawn duh skee?
for beginners/advanced	pour débutants/initiés
	poor daybewtohn/eeneesyay
How large are the groups?	Quelle est la taille des groupes?
	kehl eh lah tahy day groop?
What language are the classes in?	En quelle langue donne-t-on les leçons de ski?
	ohn kehl lohng don tawn lay luhsawn duh skee?
I'd like a lift pass, please.	Je voudrais un abonnement pour les remontées mécaniques.
	jhuh voodreh zuhn nahbonmohn poor lay ruhmawntay maykahneek
Must I give you a passport photo?	Dois-je donner une photo d'identité?
	dwah jhuh donay ewn foatoa deedohnteetay?

Where are the beginners' slopes?	Où sont les pistes de ski pour débutants?
	oo sawn lay peest duh skee poor daybewtohn?
Are there any runs for cross-country skiing?	Y a-t-il des pistes de ski de fond dans les environs?
	ee yah teel day peest duh skee duh fawn dohn lay zohnveerawn?
Have the cross-country runs been marked?	Les pistes de ski de fond, sont-elles indiquées?
	lay peest duh skee duh fawn, sawn tehl ahndeekay?
Are the...in operation?	Est-ce que les...marchent?
	ehs kuh lay...mahrsh?
– the ski lifts?	Est-ce que les remontées mécaniques marchent?
	ehs kuh lay ruhmawntay maykahneek mahrsh?
– the chair lifts?	Est-ce que les télésièges marchent?
	ehs kuh lay taylaysyehjh mahrsh?
Are the slopes usable?	Est-ce que les pistes sont ouvertes?
	ehs kuh lay peest sawn toovehrt?
Are the cross-country runs usable?	Est-ce que les pistes de ski de fond sont ouvertes?
	ehs kuh lay peest duh skee duh fawn sawn toovehrt?

13. Sickness

13.1 Call (fetch) the doctor

Could you call/fetch a doctor quickly, please?	Voulez-vous vite appeler/aller chercher un médecin s'il vous plaît? *voolay voo veet ahpuhlay/ahlay shehrshay uhn maydsahn seel voo pleh?*
When does the doctor have surgery?	Quand est-ce que le médecin reçoit? *kohn tehs kuh luh maydsahn ruhswah?*
When can the doctor come?	Quand est-ce que le médecin peut venir? *kohn tehs kuh luh maydsahn puh vuhneer?*
I'd like to make an appointment to see the doctor.	Pouvez-vous me prendre un rendez-vous chez le médecin? *poovay voo muh prohndr uhn rohnday voo shay luh maydsahn?*
I've got an appointment to see the doctor at...	J'ai un rendez-vous chez le médecin à...heures. *jhay uhn rohnday voo shay luh maydsahn a...uhr*
Which doctor/chemist has night/weekend duty?	Quel médecin/Quelle pharmacie est de garde cette nuit/ce week-end? *kehl maydsahn/kehl fahrmahsee eh duh gahrd seht nwee/suh week-ehnd?*
I have a European Health Insurance Card.	J'ai une carte de sécurité sociale européenne. *jay ewn kahrt duh saykewreetay sohseeahl uhrohpayehn*

13.2 Patient's ailments

I don't feel well.	Je ne me sens pas bien. *jhuh nuh muh sohn pah byahn*	
I'm dizzy.	J'ai des vertiges.	*jhay day vehrteejh*
– ill.	Je suis malade.	*jhuh swee mahlahd*
– sick.	J'ai mal au coeur.	*jhay mahl oa kuhr*

I've got a cold.	Je suis enrhumé(e).
	jhuh swee zohnrewmay
It hurts here.	J'ai mal ici.
	jhay mahl eesee
I've been throwing up.	J'ai vomi.
	jhay vomee
I've got…	Je souffre de…
	jhuh soofr duh…
I'm running a temperature.	J'ai de la fièvre.
	jhayduh lah fyehvr
I've been stung by a wasp.	J'ai été piqué(e) par une guêpe.
	jhay aytay peekay pahr ewn gehp
I've been stung by an insect.	J'ai été piqué(e) par un insecte.
	jhay aytay peekay pahr uhn nahnsehkt
I've been bitten by a dog.	J'ai été mordu(e) par un chien.
	jhay aytay mordew pahr uhn shyahn
I've been stung by a jellyfish.	J'ai été piqué(e) par une méduse.
	jhay aytay peekay pahr ewn maydewz
I've been bitten by a snake.	J'ai été mordu(e) par un serpent.
	jhay aytay mordew pahr uhn sehrpohn
I've been bitten by an animal.	J'ai été mordu(e) par un animal.
	jhay aytay mordew pahr uhn nahneemahl
I've cut myself.	Je me suis coupé(e).
	jhuh muh swee koopay
I've burned myself.	Je me suis brûlé(e).
	jhuh muh swee brewlay
I've grazed myself.	Je me suis égratigné(e).
	jhuh muh swee zaygrahteenyay
I've had a fall.	Je suis tombé(e).
	jhuh swee tawnbay
I've sprained my ankle.	Je me suis foulé(e) la cheville.
	jhuh muh swee foolay lah shuhveey
I've come for the morning-after pill.	Je viens pour la pilule du lendemain.
	jhuh vyahn poor lah peelewl dew lohndmahn

Quels sont vos symptômes?	What seems to be the problem?
Depuis combien de temps avez-vous ces symptômes?	How long have you had these symptoms?
Avez-vous eu ces symptômes auparavant?	Have you had this trouble before?
Avez-vous de la fièvre?	How high is your temperature?
Déshabillez-vous s'il vous plaît?	Get undressed, please.
Pouvez-vous vous mettre torse nu?	Strip to the waist, please.
Vous pouvez vous déshabiller là-bas.	You can undress there.
Pouvez-vous remonter la manche de votre bras gauche/droit?	Roll up your left/right sleeve, please.
Allongez-vous ici.	Lie down here, please.
Ceci vous fait mal?	Does this hurt?
Aspirez et expirez profondément.	Breathe deeply.
Ouvrez la bouche.	Open your mouth.

Patient's medical history

I'm a diabetic.	Je suis diabétique.
	jhuh swee dyahbayteek
I have a heart condition.	Je suis cardiaque.
	jhuh swee kahrdyahk
I have asthma.	J'ai de l'asthme.
	jhay duh lahsm
I'm allergic to...	Je suis allergique à...
	jhuh swee zahlehrjheek ah...
I'm...months pregnant.	Je suis enceinte de...mois.
	jhuh swee zohnsahnt duh...mwah

I'm on a diet.	Je suis au régime.
	jhuh swee zoa rayjheem
I'm on medication/the pill.	Je prends des médicaments/la pilule.
	jhuh prohn day maydeekahmohn/
	lah peelewl
I've had a heart attack once before.	J'ai déjà eu une crise cardiaque.
	jhay dayjhah ew ewn kreez kahrdyahk
I've had a(n)...operation.	J'ai été opéré(e) de...
	jhay aytay oapayray duh...
I've been ill recently.	Je viens d'être malade.
	jhuh vyahn dehtr mahlahd
I've got an ulcer.	J'ai un ulcère à l'estomac.
	jhay uhn newlsehr ah lehstomah
I've got my period.	J'ai mes règles.
	jhay may rehgl

☞

Avez-vous des allergies?	Do you have any allergies?
Prenez-vous des médicaments?	Are you on any medication?
Suivez-vous un régime?	Are you on any sort of diet?
Etes-vous enceinte?	Are you pregnant?
Etes-vous vacciné(e) contre le tétanos?	Have you had a tetanus vaccination?

The diagnosis

Is it contagious?	Est-ce contagieux?
	ehs kawntahjhyuh?
How long do I have to stay...?	Combien de temps dois-je rester...?
	kawnbyahn duh tohn dwah jhuh
	rehstay...?
– in bed?	Combien de temps dois-je rester au lit?
	kawnbyahn duh tohn dwah jhuh rehstay
	oa lee?

- in hospital?	Combien de temps dois-je rester à l'hôpital?
	kawnbyahn duh tohn dwah jhuh rehstay ah loapeetahl?
Do I have to go on a special diet?	Dois-je suivre un régime?
	dwah jhuh sweevr uhn rayjheem?
Am I allowed to travel?	Puis-je voyager?
	pwee jhuh vwahyahjhay?
Can I make a new appointment?	Puis-je prendre un autre rendez-vous?
	pwee jhuh prohndr uhn noatr rohnday voo?
When do I have to come back?	Quand dois-je revenir?
	kohn dwah jhuh ruhvuhneer?
I'll come back tomorrow.	Je reviendrai demain.
	jhuh ruhvyahndray duhmahn

☞

Ce n'est rien de grave.	It's nothing serious.
Vous vous êtes cassé le/la...	Your...is broken.
Vous vous êtes foulé le/la...	You've sprained your...
Vous vous êtes déchiré le/la...	You've got a torn...
Vous avez une inflammation.	You've got an inflammation.
Vous avez une crise d'appendicite.	You've got appendicitis.
Vous avez une bronchite.	You've got bronchitis.
Vous avez une maladie vénérienne.	You've got a venereal disease.
Vous avez une grippe.	You've got the flu.
Vous avez eu une crise cardiaque.	You've had a heart attack.
Vous avez une infection (virale/bactérielle).	You've got an infection (viral/bacterial).
Vous avez une pneumonie.	You've got pneumonia.
Vous avez un ulcère à l'estomac.	You've got an ulcer.

Vous vous êtes froissé un muscle.	You've pulled a muscle.
Vous avez une infection vaginale.	You've got a vaginal infection.
Vous avez une intoxication alimentaire.	You've got food poisoning.
Vous avez une insolation.	You've got sunstroke.
Vous êtes allergique à...	You're allergic to...
Vous êtes enceinte.	You're pregnant.
Je veux faire analyser votre sang/urine/vos selles.	I'd like to have your blood/urine/ stools tested.
Il faut faire des points de suture.	It needs stitching.
Je vous envoie à un spécialiste/ l'hôpital.	I'm referring you to a specialist/ sending you to hospital.
Il faut faire des radios.	You'll need to have some x-rays taken.
Voulez-vous reprendre place un petitinstant dans la salle d'attente?	Could you wait in the waiting room, please?
Il faut vous opérer.	You'll need an operation.
Vous devez revenir demain/ dans...jours.	Come back tomorrow/ in...days' time.

How do I take this medicine?	Comment dois-je prendre ces médicaments?
	komohn dwah jhuh prohndr say maydeekahmohn?
How many capsules/drops/ injections/spoonfuls/ tablets each time?	Combien de capsules/gouttes/piqûres/ cuillères/comprimés à chaque fois?
	kawnbyahn duh kahpsewl/goot/ peekewr/kweeyehr/kawnpreemay ah shahk fwah?
How many times a day?	Combien de fois par jour?
	kawnbyahn duh fwah pahr jhoor?
I've forgotten my medication. At home I take...	J'ai oublié mes médicaments. A la maison je prends...
	jhay oobleeyay may maydeekahmohn. ah lah mehzawn jhuh prohn...
Could you make out a prescription for me?	Pouvez-vous me faire une ordonnance?
	poovay voo muh fehr ewn ordonohns?

avaler entièrement
swallow whole

avant chaque repas
before meals

capsules
capsules

la prise de ce médicament peut rendre dangereuse la conduite automobile
this medication impairs your driving

comprimés
tablets

cuillerées (...à soupe/...à café)
spoonfuls (tablespoons/ teaspoons)

dissoudre dans l'eau
dissolve in water

enduire
rub on

finir le traitement
finish the course

...fois par jour
...times a day

gouttes
drops

pendant...jours
for...days

piqûres
injections

pommade
ointment

prendre
take

toutes les...heures
every...hours

uniquement pour usage externe
not for internal use

155

Je vous prescris un antibiotique/ un sirop/un tranquillisant/ un calmant.	I'm prescribing antibiotics/a mixture/a tranquillizer/pain killer.
Vous devez rester au calme.	Have lots of rest.
Vous ne devez pas sortir.	Stay indoors.
Vous devez rester au lit.	Stay in bed.

13.5 At the dentist's

Do you know a good dentist?	Connaissez-vous un bon dentiste?
	konehsay voo zuhn bawn dohnteest?
Could you make a dentist's appointment for me? It's urgent.	Pouvez-vous me prendre un rendez-vous chez le dentiste? C'est urgent.
	poovay voo muh prohndr uhn rohnday voo shay luh dohnteest? seh tewrjhohn
Can I come in today, please?	Puis-je venir aujourd'hui s'il vous plaît?
	pwee jhuh vuhneer oajhoordwee seel voo pleh?
I have (terrible) toothache.	J'ai une rage de dents/un mal de dents (épouvantable).
	jhay ewn rahjh duh dohn/uhn mahl duh dohn (aypoovohntahbl)
Could you prescribe/ give me a painkiller?	Pouvez-vous me prescrire/donner un calmant?
	poovay voo muh prehskreer/donay uhn kahlmohn?
A piece of my tooth has broken off.	Ma dent s'est cassée.
	mah dohn seh kahssay
My filling's come out.	Mon plombage est parti.
	mawn plawnbahjh eh pahrtee

've got a broken crown.	Ma couronne est cassée.
	mah kooron eh kahssay
'd like/I don't want a local anaesthetic.	Je (ne) veux (pas) une anesthésie locale.
	jhuh (nuh) vuh (paz) ewn ahnehstayzee lokahl
Can you do a makeshift repair job?	Pouvez-vous me soigner de façon provisoire?
	poovay voo muh swahnyay duh fahsawn proveezwahr?
don't want this tooth pulled.	Je ne veux pas que cette dent soit arrachée.
	jhuh nuh vuh pah kuh seht dohn swaht ahrahshay
My dentures are broken. Can you fix them?	Mon dentier est cassé. Pouvez-vous le réparer?
	mawn dohntyay eh kahssay. poovay voo luh raypahray?

☞

Quelle dent/molaire vous fait mal?	Which tooth hurts?
Vous avez un abcès.	You've got an abscess.
Je dois faire une dévitalisation.	I'll have to do a root canal.
Je vais vous faire une anesthésie locale.	I'm giving you a local anaesthetic.
Je dois plomber/extraire/polir cette dent.	I'll have to fill/pull/file this tooth.
Je dois utiliser la roulette.	I'll have to drill.
Ouvrez bien la bouche.	Open your mouth.
Fermez la bouche.	Close your mouth.
Rincez.	Rinse.
Sentez-vous encore la douleur?	Does it hurt still?

14. In trouble

Help!	Au secours!	*oa suhkoor!*
Fire!	Au feu!	*oa fuh!*
Police!	Police!	*pohlees!*
Quick!	Vite!	*veet!*
Danger!	Danger!	*dohnjhay*
Watch out!	Attention!	*ahtohnsyawn!*
Stop!	Stop!	*stop!*
Be careful!	Prudence!	*prewdohns!*
Don't!	Arrêtez!	*ahrehtay!*
Let go!	Lâchez!	*lahshay!*
Stop that thief!	Au voleur!	*oa voluhr!*

Could you help me, please? Voulez-vous m'aider?
voolay voo mayday?

Where's the police station/ Où est le poste de police/la sortie
emergency exit/fire escape? de secours/l'escalier de secours?
*oo eh luh post duh polees/lah sortee
duh suhkoor/lehskahlyay duh suhkoor?*

Where's the nearest Où y a-t-il un extincteur?
fire extinguisher? *oo ee yah teel uhn nehxtahnktuhr?*

Call the fire brigade! Prévenez les sapeurs-pompiers!
prayvuhnay lay sahpuhr pawnpyay!

Call the police! Appelez la police!
ahpuhlay lah polees!

Call an ambulance! Appelez une ambulance!
ahpuhlay ewn ohnbewlohns!

Where's the nearest phone? Où est le téléphone le plus proche?
oo eh luh taylayfon luh plew prosh?

Could I use your phone? Puis-je utiliser votre téléphone?
pwee jhuh ewteeleezay votr taylayfon?

What's the emergency Quel est le numéro d'urgence?
number? *kehl eh luh newmayroa dewrjhohns?*

What's the number for Quel est le numéro de téléphone
the police? de la police?
*kehl eh luh newmayroa duh taylayfon
duh lah polees?*

14.2 Loss

I've lost my purse/wallet/ mobile phone/passport.	J'ai perdu mon porte-monnaie/ portefeuille/téléphone portable/ passeport.
	jhay pehrdew mawn port moneh/ portfuhy/taylayfohn pohrtahbl/ pahspohr
I lost my...yesterday.	Hier j'ai oublié mon/ma...
	yehr jhay oobleeay mawn/mah...
I left my...here.	J'ai laissé mon/ma...ici.
	jhay layssay mawn/mah...eesee
Did you find my...?	Avez-vous trouvé mon/ma...?
	ahvay voo troovay mawn/mah...?
It was right here.	Il était là.
	eel ayteh lah
It's quite valuable.	C'est un objet de valeur.
	seh tuhn nobjheh duh vahluhr
Where's the lost property office?	Où est le bureau des objets trouvés?
	oo eh luh bewroa day zobjheh troovay?

14.3 Accidents

There's been an accident.	Il y a eu un accident.
	eel ee yah ew uhn nahkseedohn
Someone's fallen into the water.	Quelqu'un est tombé dans l'eau.
	kehlkuhn eh tawnbay dohn loa
There's a fire.	Il y a un incendie.
	eel ee yah uhn nahnsohndee
Is anyone hurt?	Y a-t-il quelqu'un de blessé?
	ee yah teel kehlkuhn duh blehssay?
Some people have been/ no one's been injured.	Il (n)y a des(pas de) blessés.
	eel (n)ee yah day(pah duh) blehssay

There's someone in the car/train still.	Il y a encore quelqu'un dans la voiture/le train.
	eel ee ah ohnkor kehlkuhn dohn lah vwahtewr/luh trahn
It's not too bad. Don't worry.	Ce n'est pas si grave. Ne vous inquiétez pas.
	suh neh pah see grahv. nuh voo zahnkyaytay pah
Leave everything the way it is, please.	Ne touchez à rien s'il vous plaît.
	nuh tooshay ah ryahn seel voo pleh
I want to talk to the police first.	Je veux d'abord parler à la police.
	jhuh vuh dahbor pahrlay ah lah polees
I want to take a photo first.	Je veux d'abord prendre une photo.
	jhuh vuh dahbor prohndr ewn foatoa
Here's my name and address.	Voici mon nom et mon adresse.
	vwahsee mawn nawn ay mawn nahdrehs
Could I have your name and address?	Puis-je connaître votre nom et votre adresse?
	pwee jhuh konehtr votr nawn ay votr ahdrehs?
Could I see some identification/your insurance papers?	Puis-je voir vos papiers d'identité/ papiers d'assurance?
	pwee jhuh vwahr voa pahpyay deedohnteetay/pahpyay dahsewrohns?
Will you act as a witness?	Voulez-vous être témoin?
	voolay voo zehtr taymwahn?
I need the details for the insurance.	Je dois avoir les données pour l'assurance.
	jhuh dwah zahvwahr lay donay poor lahsewrohns
Are you insured?	Etes-vous assuré?
	eht voo zahsewray?
Third party or comprehensive?	Responsabilité civile ou tous risques?
	rehspawnsahbeeleetay seeveel oo too reesk?

Could you sign here, please? Voulez-vous signer ici?
voolay voo seenyay eesee?

14.4 Theft

I've been robbed. On m'a volé. *awn mah volay*
My...has been stolen. Mon/ma...a été volé(e).
mawn/mah...ah aytay volay
My car's been broken into. On a cambriolé ma voiture.
awn nah kohnbreeolay mah vwahtewr
My room has been On a forcé la porte de ma chambre.
broken into. *awn a fohrsay lah pohrt duh mah shohnbr*

14.5 Missing person

I've lost my child/ J'ai perdu mon enfant/ma grand-mère.
grandmother. *jhay pehrdew mawn nohnfohn/mah
grohnmehr*
Could you help me find Voulez-vous m'aider à le/la chercher?
him/her? *voolay voo mayday ah luh/lah
shehrshay?*
Have you seen a small child? Avez-vous vu un petit enfant?
ahvay voo vew uhn puhtee tohnfohn?
He's/she's...years old. Il/elle a...ans. *eel/ehl ah...ohn*
He's/she's got short/long/ Il/elle a les cheveux courts/longs/
blond/red/brown/black/ blonds/ roux/bruns/noirs/
grey/curly/ straight/ gris/bouclés/raides/frisés.
frizzy hair. *eel/ehl ah lay shuhvuh koor/lawn/blawn/
roo/bruhn/nwahr/gree/rehd/freezay*
with a ponytail avec une queue de cheval
ahvehk ewn kuh duh shuhvahl
with plaits avec des nattes
ahvehk day naht
in a bun avec un chignon
ahvehk uhn sheenyawn

He's/she's got blue/brown/ green eyes.	Il/elle a les yeux bleus/bruns/verts. *eel/ehl ah lay zyuh bluh/bruhn/vehr*
He's wearing swimming trunks/mountaineering boots.	Il porte un maillot de bain/des chaussures de montagne. *eel port uhn mahyoa duh bahn/day shoasewr duh mawntahnyuh*
with/without glasses/a bag	avec/sans lunettes/un sac *ahvehk/sohn lewneht/uhn sahk*
tall/short	grand(e)/petit(e) *grohn(d)/puhtee(t)*
This is a photo of him/her.	Voici une photo de lui/d'elle. *vwahsee ewn foatoa duh lwee/dehl*
He/she must be lost.	Il/elle s'est certainement égaré(e). *eel/ehl seh sehrtehnmohn aygahray*

14.6 The police

An arrest

Vos papiers de voiture s'il vous plaît.	Your registration papers, please.
Vous rouliez trop vite.	You were speeding.
Vous devez faire un alcootest.	You are required to give a breath test.
Vous êtes en stationnement interdit.	You're not allowed to park here.
Vous n'avez pas mis d'argent dans le parcmètre.	You haven't put money in the meter.
Vos phares ne marchent pas.	Your lights aren't working.
Vous avez une contravention de...Euros.	That's a... Euros fine.
Vous voulez payer immédiatement?	Do you want to pay on the spot?
Vous devez payer immédiatement.	You'll have to pay on the spot.

I don't speak French.	Je ne parle pas français.
	jhuh nuh pahrl pah frohnseh
I didn't see the sign.	Je n'ai pas vu ce panneau.
	jhuh nay pah vew suh pahnoa
I don't understand what it says.	Je ne comprends pas ce qu'il y est écrit.
	jhuh nuh kawnprohn pah suh keel ee yeh taykree
I was only doing...kilometres an hour.	Je ne roulais qu'à...kilomètres à l'heure.
	jhuh nuh rooleh kah...keeloamehtr ah luhr
I'll have my car checked.	Je vais faire réviser ma voiture.
	jhuh veh fehr rayveezay mah vwahtewr
I was blinded by oncoming lights.	J'ai été aveuglé(e) par une voiture en sens inverse.
	jhay aytay ahvuhglay pahr ewn vwahtewr ohn sohns ahnvehrs

At the police station

Où est-ce arrivé?	Where did it happen?
Qu'avez-vous perdu?	What's missing?
Qu'a-t-on volé?	What's been taken?
Puis-je voir vos papiers d'identité?	Do you have some identification?
A quelle heure est-ce arrivé?	What time did it happen?
Qui est en cause?	Who are the others?
Y a-t-il des témoins?	Are there any witnesses?
Voulez-vous remplir ceci?	Fill this out, please
Signez ici s'il vous plaît	Sign here, please
Voulez-vous un interprète?	Do you want an interpreter?

want to report a collision/ missing person/rape/ robbery/mugging/assault.

Je viens faire la déclaration d'une collision/d'une disparition/d'un viol/un vol/un racket/une agression.

jhuh vyahn fehr lah dayklahrasyawn dewn koleezyawn/dewn deespahreesyawn/ duhn vyol/ahn vohl/ahn rahkeht/ewn agrehseeawn

Could you make out a report, please?

Voulez-vous faire un rapport?

voolay voo fehr uhn rahpor?

Could I have a copy for the insurance?

Puis-je avoir une copie pour l'assurance?

pwee jhahvwahr ewn kopee poor lahsewrohns?

I've lost everything.

J'ai tout perdu.

jhay too pehrdew

I'd like an interpreter.

J'aimerais un interprète.

jhehmuhreh zuhn nahntehrpreht

I'm innocent.

Je suis innocent(e).

jhuh swee zeenosohn(t)

I don't know anything about it.

Je ne sais rien.

jhuh nuh seh ryahn

I want to speak to someone from the British consulate.

Je veux parler à quelqu'un du consulat britannique.

jhuh vuh pahrlay ah kehlkuhn dew kawnsewlah breetahneek

I need to see someone from the British embassy.

Je dois parler à quelqu'un de l'ambassade britannique.

jhuh dwah pahrlay ah kehlkuhn duh lohnbahsahd breetahneek

I want a lawyer who speaks English.

Je veux un avocat qui parle anglais.

jhuh vuh uhn nahvokah kee pahrl ohngleh

15. Word list

Word list English–French

● This word list supplements the previous chapters. Nouns are always accompanied by the French definite article in order to indicate whether it is a masculine (*le*) or feminine (*la*) word. In the case of an abbreviated article (*l'*), the gender is indicated by (m.) or (f.). In a number of cases, words not contained in this list can be found elsewhere in this book, namely in the lists of the parts of the car and the bicycle (both **Section 5**) and the tent (**Section 7**). Many food terms can be found in the Menu reader in **Section 4.7**.

A

a little	un peu	*uhn puh*
about	environ	*ohnveerawn*
above	au-dessus	*oadsew*
abroad	l'étranger (m.)	*laytrohnjhay*
accident	l'accident (m.)	*lahkseedohn*
adder	la vipère	*lah veepehr*
addition	l'addition (f.)	*lahdeesyawn*
address	l'adresse (f.)	*lahdrehs*
admission	l'entrée (f.)	*lohntray*
admission price	le prix d'entrée	*luh pree dohntray*
advice	le conseil	*luh kawnsehy*
after	après	*ahpreh*
afternoon	l'après-midi (m., f.)	*lahpreh meedee*
aftershave	la lotion après-rasage	*lah loasyawn ahpreh rahzahjh*
again	à nouveau	*ah noovoa*
against	contre	*kawntr*
age	l'âge (m.)	*lahjh*
air conditioning	l'air conditionné (m.)	*lehr kawndeesyonay*
air mattress	le matelas pneumatique	*luh mahtlah pnuhmahteek*
air sickness bag	le petit sac à vomissements	*luh puhtee sahk ah vomeesmohn*
aircraft	l'avion (m.)	*lahvyawn*

airport	l'aéroport (m.)	*lahayroapor*
alarm	l'alarme (f.)	*lahlahrm*
alarm clock	le réveil	*luh rayvehy*
alcohol	l'alcool (m.)	*lahlkol*
A-level equivalent	le bac	*luh bahk*
allergic	allergique	*ahlehrjheek*
alone	seul	*suhl*
always	toujours	*toojhoor*
ambulance	l'ambulance (f.)	*lohnbewlohns*
amount	le montant	*luh mawntohn*
amusement park	le parc d'attractions	*luh pahrk dahtrahksyawn*
anaesthetize	anesthésier	*ahnehstayzyay*
anchovy	l'anchois (m.)	*lohnshwah*
and	et	*ay*
angry	en colère	*ohn kolehr*
animal	l'animal (m.)	*lahneemahl*
answer	la réponse	*lah raypawns*
ant	la fourmi	*lah foormee*
antibiotics	l'antibiotique (m.)	*lohnteebyoteek*
antifreeze	l'antigel (m.)	*lohnteejhehl*
antique	ancien	*ohnsyahn*
antiques	antiquités (f.)	*ohnteekeetay*
antiseptic cream	crème antiseptique	*crehm ohnteesehpteek*
anus	l'anus (m.)	*lahnews*
apartment	l'appartement (m.)	*lahpahrtuhmohn*
aperitif	l'apéritif (m.)	*lahpayreeteef*
apologies	les excuses	*lay zehxkewz*
apple	la pomme	*lah pom*
apple juice	le jus de pommes	*luh jhew duh pom*
apple pie	la tarte aux pommes	*lah tahrt oa pom*
apple sauce	la compote de pommes	*lah kawnpot duh pom*
appointment	le rendez-vous	*luh rohndayvoo*
apricot	l'abricot (m.)	*lahbreekoa*
April	avril	*ahvreel*
archbishop	l'archevêque (m.)	*lahrshuhvehk*
architecture	l'architecture (f.)	*lahrsheetehktewr*
area	les environs	*lay zohnveerawn*

arm	le bras	*luh brah*
arrive	arriver	*ahreevay*
arrow	la flèche	*lah flehsh*
art	l'art (m.)	*lahr*
artery	l'artère (f.)	*lahrtehr*
artichoke	l'artichaut (m.)	*lahrteeshoa*
article	l'article (m.)	*lahrteekl*
artificial respiration	la respiration artificielle	*lah rehspeerahsawn ahrteefeesyehl*
arts and crafts	l'artisanat d'art	*lahrteezahnah dahr*
ashtray	le cendrier	*luh sohndreeay*
ask	demander	*duhmohnday*
ask	prier	*preeay*
asparagus	les asperges	*lay zahspehrjh*
aspirin	l'aspirine (f.)	*lahspeereen*
assault	l'agression (f.)	*lahgrehsyawn*
at home	à la maison	*ah lah mehzawn*
at night	la nuit	*lah nwee*
at the back	à l'arrière	*ah lahryehr*
at the front	à l'avant	*ah lahvohn*
at the latest	au plus tard	*oa plew tahr*
aubergine	l'aubergine (f.)	*loabehrjheen*
August	aôut	*oot*
automatic	automatique	*loatoamahteek*
automatically	automatiquement	*oatoamahteekmohn*
autumn	l'automne (m.)	*loatonn*
avalanche	l'avalanche (f.)	*lahvahlohnsh*
awake	réveillé	*rayvay-yay*
awning	le parasol	*luh pahrahsol*

B

baby	le bébé	*luh baybay*
baby food	la nourriture pour bébé	*lah nooreetewr poor baybay*
babysitter	le/la baby-sitter	*luh/lah behbee seetehr*
back	le dos	*luh doa*

backpack	le sac à dos	*luh sahk ah doa*
bacon	le lard	*luh lahr*
bad	mauvais	*moaveh*
bag	le sac	*luh sahk*
baker (cakes)	le pâtissier	*luh pahteesyay*
baker	le boulanger	*luh boolohnjhay*
balcony (theatre)	le balcon	*luh bahlkawn*
balcony (to building)	le balcon	*luh bahlkawn*
ball	la balle	*lah bahl*
ballet	le ballet; la danse	*luh bahleh; la dohns*
ballpoint pen	le stylo à bille	*luh steeloa ah beey*
banana	la banane	*lah bahnahn*
bandage	le pansement	*luh pohnsmohn*
bank (river)	la rive	*lah reev*
bank	la banque	*lah bohnk*
bank card	la carte bancaire	*lah kahrt bohnkehr*
bar (café)	le bar	*luh bahr*
bar (drinks' cabinet)	le bar	*luh bahr*
barbecue	le barbecue	*luh bahrbuhkew*
bath	le bain	*luh bahn*
bath attendant	le maître nageur	*luh mehtr nahjhuhr*
bath foam	la mousse de bain	*lah moos duh bahn*
bath towel	la serviette de bain	*lah sehrvyeht duh bahn*
bathing cap	le bonnet de bain	*luh boneh duh bahn*
bathing cubicle	la cabine de bain	*lah kahbeen duh bahn*
bathing costume	le maillot de bain	*luh mahyoa duh bahn*
bathroom	la salle de bain	*lah sahl duh bahn*
battery (car)	l'accumulateur (m.)	*lahkewmewlahtuhr*
battery	la pile	*lah peel*
beach	la plage	*lah plahjh*
beans	les haricots	*lay ahreekoa*
beautiful	beau/belle/magnifique	*boa/behl/mahnyeefeek*
beauty parlour	le salon de beauté	*luh sahlawn duh boatay*
bed	le lit	*luh lee*
bee	l'abeille (f.)	*lahbehy*
beef	la viande de boeuf	*lah vyohnd duh buhf*
beer	la bière	*lah byehr*

beetroot	la betterave	*lah behtrahv*
begin	commencer	*komohnsay*
beginner	le débutant	*luh daybewtohn*
behind	derrière	*dehryehr*
Belgian (f)	la belge	*lah behljh*
Belgian (m)	le belge	*luh behljh*
Belgium	la Belgique	*lah behljheek*
belt	la ceinture	*lah sahntewr*
berth	la couchette	*lah koosheht*
better	mieux	*myuh*
bicarbonate of soda	le bicarbonate de soude	*luh beekahrbonaht duh sood*
bicycle	la bicyclette/le vélo	*lah beeseekleht/luh vayloa*
bicycle pump	la pompe à bicyclettelah	*pawnp ah beeseekleht*
bicycle repairman	le réparateur de vélos	*luh raypahrahtuhr duh vayloa*
bikini	le bikini	*luh beekeenee*
bill	l'addition	*lahdeesyawn*
birthday	l'anniversaire (m.)	*lahneevehrsehr*
biscuit	le biscuit	*luh beeskwee*
bite	mordre	*mordr*
bitter	amer	*ahmehr*
black	noir	*nwahr*
bland	fade	*fahd*
blanket	la couverture	*lah koovehrtewr*
bleach	blondir	*blawndeer*
blister	la cloque	*lah klok*
blond	blond	*blawn*
blood	le sang	*luh sohn*
blood pressure	la tension	*lah tohnsyawn*
blouse	le chemisier	*luh shuhmeezyay*
blow dry	sécher	*sayshay*
blue	bleu	*bluh*
blunt	épointé/émoussé	*aypwahntay/aymoosay*
boat	le bateau	*luh bahtoa*
body	le corps	*luh kor*

body milk	le lait corporel	*luh leh korporehl*
boil	bouillir	*boo-yeer*
boiled	cuit	*kwee*
boiled ham	jambon cuit	*jhohnbawn kwee*
bone	l'os (m.)	*los*
bonnet	le capot	*luh kahpoa*
book (verb)	réserver	*raysehrvay*
book	le livre	*luh leevr*
booked	réservé	*rayzehrvay*
booking office	le bureau de	*luh bewroa duh*
	réservation	*rayzehrvahsyawn*
bookshop	la librairie	*lah leebrehree*
border	la frontière	*lah frawntyehr*
bored (to be)	s'ennuyer	*sonweeyay*
boring	ennuyeux	*onweeyuh*
born	né	*nay*
botanical gardens	le jardin botanique	*luh jhahrdahn botahneek*
both	tous/toutes les deux	*too/toot lay duh*
bottle-warmer	le chauffe-biberon	*luh shoaf beebrawn*
bottle (baby's)	le biberon	*luh beebrawn*
bottle	la bouteille	*lah bootehy*
box	la boîte	*lah bwaht*
box (theatre)	la loge	*lah lojh*
boy	le garçon	*luh gahrsawn*
bra	le soutien-gorge	*luh sootyahn gorjh*
bracelet	le bracelet	*luh brahsleh*
braised	braisé	*brehzay*
brake	le frein	*luh frahn*
brake fluid	le liquide de freins	*luh leekeed duh frahn*
brake oil	l'huile à frein (f.)	*lweel ah frahn*
bread	le pain	*luh pahn*
break	casser	*kahssay*
breakfast	le petit déjeuner	*luh puhtee dayjhuhnay*
breast	la poitrine	*lah pwahtreen*
bridge	le pont	*luh pawn*
briefs	la culotte	*lah kewlot*
brochure	la brochure	*lah broshewr*

broken	cassé	kahssay
broth	le consommé	luh kawnsomay
brother	le frère	luh frehr
brown	brun	bruhn
brush	la brosse	lah bros
Brussels sprouts	les choux de Bruxelles	lay shoo duh brewxehl
bucket	le seau	luh soa
bugs	les insectes nuisibles	lay zahnsehkt nweezeebl
building	le bâtiment	luh bahteemohn
buoy	la bouée	lah booway
burglary	le cambriolage	luh kohnbryolajh
burn (verb)	brûler	brewlay
burn	la brûlure	lah brewlewr
burnt	brûlé	brewlay
bus	l'autobus (m.)	loatoabews
bus station	la station d'autobus	lah stahsyawn doatoabews
bus stop	l'arrêt d'autobus (m.)	lahreh doatoabews
business class	la classe affaire (f.)	lah klahs ahfehr
business trip	le voyage d'affaires	luh vwahyahjh dahfehr
busy	animé	ahneemay
butane gas	le gaz butane	luh gahz bewtahnn
butcher	le boucher	luh booshay
butter	le beurre	luh buhr
button	le bouton	luh bootawn
buy	acheter	ahshtay
by airmail	la poste aérienne/ par avion	lah post ahayryehn/ pahr ahvyawn

C

cabbage	le chou	luh shoo
cabin	la cabine	lah kahbeen
cake	le gâteau	luh gahtoa
call	appeler	ahpuhlay
called (to be)	s'appeler	sahpuhlay
camera	l'appareil-photo (m.)	lahpahrehy foatoa
camp	faire du camping	fehr dew kohnpeeng

camp shop	le magasin du camping	*luh mahgahzahn dew kohnpeeng*
camp site	le camping	*luh kohnpeeng*
camper	le camping-car	*luh kohnpeeng kahr*
campfire	le feu de camp	*luh fuh duh kohn*
camping guide	le guide de camping	*luh gueed duh kohnpeeng*
camping permit	le permis de camping	*luh pehrmee duh kohnpeeng*
canal boat	la péniche	*lah payneesh*
cancel	annuler	*ahnewlay*
candle	la bougie	*lah boojhee*
canoe (verb)	faire du canoë	*fehr dew kahnoaeh*
canoe	le canoë	*luh kahnoaeh*
car (train)	le wagon	*luh vahgawn*
car	la voiture	*lah vwahtewr*
car deck	le pont à voitures	*luh pawn ah vwahtewr*
car documents	les papiers de voiture	*lay pahpyay duh vwahtewr*
car trouble	la panne	*lah pahnn*
carafe	la carafe	*lah kahrahf*
caravan	la caravane	*lah kahrahvahnn*
cardigan	le cardigan/le gilet	*luh kahrdeegahn/luh jheeleh*
careful	prudent	*prewdohn*
carrot	la carotte	*lah kahrot*
cartridge	la cartouche	*lah kahrtoosh*
cartridge	la cassette	*lah kahseht*
cascade	la cascade	*lah kahskahd*
cash desk	la caisse	*lah kehss*
casino	le casino	*luh kahzeenoa*
cassette	la cassette	*lah kahseht*
castle	le château	*luh shahtoa*
cat	le chat	*luh shah*
catalogue	le catalogue	*luh kahtahlog*
cathedral	la cathédrale	*lah kahtaydrahl*
cauliflower	le chou-fleur	*luh shoo fluhr*
cave	la grotte	*lah grot*
CD	le compact disc	*luh kawnpahkt deesk*

celebrate	célébrer	*saylaybray*
cellotape	le scotch	*luh skoch*
cemetery	le cimetière	*luh seemtyehr*
centimetre	le centimètre	*luh sohnteemehtr*
central heating	le chauffage central	*luh shoafahjh sohntrahl*
centre (in the)	au milieu	*oa meelyuh*
centre	le centre	*luh sohntr*
cereal	la céréale	*lah sayrayahl*
chair	la chaise	*lah shehz*
chambermaid	la femme de chambre	*lah fahm duh shohnbr*
chamois	la peau de chamois	*lah poa duh shahmwah*
champagne	le champagne	*luh shohnpany*
change (verb)	modifier, changer	*modeefyay, shohnjhay*
change	la monnaie	*lah moneh*
change the baby's nappy	changer la couche du bébé	*shohnjhay lah koosh dew baybay*
change the oil	changer l'huile	*shohnjhay lweel*
chapel	la chapelle	*lah shahpehl*
charter flight	le vol charter	*luh vol shahrtehr*
chat up	draguer	*drahgay*
check (verb)	contrôler	*kawntroalay*
check in	enregistrer	*ohnruhjheestray*
cheers	à votre santé	*ah votr sohntay*
cheese	le fromage	*luh fromahjh*
chef	le chef	*luh shehf*
chemist	la pharmacie	*lah fahrmahsee*
cheque	le chèque	*luh shehk*
cherries	les cerises	*lay suhreez*
chess (play)	jouer aux échecs	*jhooay oa zayshehk*
chewing gum	le chewing-gum	*luh shweenguhm*
chicken	le poulet	*luh pooleh*
chicory	les endives	*lay zohndeev*
child	l'enfant (m./f.)	*lohnfohn*
child seat	le siège-enfant	*luh seeyehjh ohnfohn*
chilled	rafraîchi	*rahfrehshee*
chin	le menton	*luh montawn*
chips	les pommes-frites	*lay pom freet*

chocolate	le chocolat	*luh shoakoalah*
choose	choisir	*shwahzeer*
chop	la côtelette	*lah koatuhleht*
christian name	le prénom	*luh praynawn*
church	l'église (f.)	*laygleez*
church service	le service religieux	*luh sehrvees ruhleejhyuh*
cigar	le cigare	*luh seegahr*
cigar shop	le tabac	*luh tahbah*
cigarette	la cigarette	*lah seegahreht*
cigarette paper	le papier à cigarettes	*luh pahpay ah seegahreht*
circle	le cercle	*luh sehrkl*
circus	le cirque	*luh seerk*
city	la ville	*lah veel*
map	le plan	*luh plohn*
classical concert	le concert classique	*luh kawnsehr klahsseek*
clean (verb)	nettoyer	*nehtwahyay*
clean	propre	*propr*
clear	clair	*klehr*
clearance	les soldes	*lay sold*
closed	fermé	*fehrmay*
closed off	bloqué	*blokay*
clothes	les habits	*lay zahbee*
clothes hanger	le cintre	*luh sahntr*
clothes peg	la pince à linge	*lah pahns ah lahnjh*
clothing	vêtements	*vehtmohn*
coach	l'autobus (m.)	*loatoabews*
coat	le manteau	*luh mohntoa*
cockroach	le cafard	*luh kahfahr*
cocoa	le cacao	*luh kahkahoa*
cod	le cabillaud	*luh kahbeeyoa*
coffee	le café	*luh kahfay*
coffee filter	le filtre de cafetière	*luh feeltr duh kahftyehr*
cognac	le cognac	*luh konyahk*
cold	froid	*frwah*
cold	le rhume	*luh rewm*
cold cuts	la charcuterie	*lah shahrkewtree*
collarbone	la clavicule	*lah klahveekewl*

colleague	le collègue	*luh kolehg*
collision	la collision	*lah koleezyawn*
cologne	l'eau de toilette (f.)	*loa duh twahleht*
colour	la couleur	*lah kooluhr*
colour pencils	les crayons de couleur	*lay krayawn duh kooluhr*
colouring book	l'album de coloriage (m.)	*lahlbuhm duh koloryajh*
comb	le peigne	*luh pehnyuh*
come	venir	*vuhneer*
come back	revenir	*ruhvuhneer*
compartment	le compartiment	*luh kawnpahrteemohn*
complaint	la plainte	*lah plahnt*
completely	entièrement	*ohntyehrmohn*
compliment	le compliment	*luh kawnpleemohn*
compulsory	obligatoire	*obleegahtwahr*
computer	ordinateur	*ohrdeenahtuhr*
concert	le concert	*luh kawnsehr*
concert hall	la salle de concert	*lah sahl duh kawnsehr*
concussion	la commotion cérébrale	*lah koamoasyawn sayraybrahl*
condensed milk	le lait condensé	*luh leh kawndohnsay*
condom	le préservatif	*luh prayzehrvahteef*
congratulate	féliciter	*fayleeseetay*
connection	la liaison	*lah lyehzawn*
constipation	la constipation	*lah kawnsteepahsyawn*
consulate	le consulat	*luh kownsewlah*
consultation	la consultation	*lah kawnsewltahsyawn*
contact lens	la lentille de contact	*lah lohnteey duh kawntahkt*
contact lens solution	le liquide pour lentille de contact	*luh leekeed poor lohnteey duh kawntahkt*
contagious	contagieux	*kawntahjhyuh*
contraceptive	le contraceptif	*luh kawntrahsehpteef*
contraceptive pill	la pilule anticonceptionnelle	*lah peelewl ohnteekawn-sehpsyonehl*
convent	le couvent	*luh koovohn*
cook (verb)	cuisiner	*kweezeenay*
cook	le cuisinier	*luh kweezeenyay*

copper	le cuivre	*luh kweevr*
copy	la copie	*lah kopee*
corkscrew	le tire-bouchon	*luh teerbooshawn*
cornflour	la maïzena	*lah maheezaynah*
corner	le coin	*luh kwahn*
correct	correct	*korehkt*
correspond	correspondre	*korehspawndr*
corridor	le couloir	*luh koolwahr*
costume	le costume	*luh kostewm*
cot	le lit d'enfant	*luh lee dohnfohn*
cotton	le coton	*luh koatawn*
cotton wool	le coton	*luh koatawn*
cough	la toux	*lah too*
cough mixture	le sirop pectoral	*luh seeroa pehktoaral*
counter	la réception	*lah raysehpsyawn*
country	le pays	*luh pehy*
country	la campagne	*lah kohnpahnyuh*
country code	l'indicatif du pays (m.)	*lahndeekahteef dew pehy*
courgette	la courgette	*lah koorjheht*
cousin (f)	la cousine	*lah koozeen*
cousin (m)	le cousin	*luh koozahn*
crab	le crabe	*luh krahb*
cream	la crème	*lah krehm*
credit card	la carte de crédit	*lah kahrt duh kraydee*
crisps	les chips	*lay sheeps*
croissant	le croissant	*luh krwahssohn*
cross-country run	la piste de ski de fond	*lah peest duh skeeduh fawn*
cross-country skiing	faire du ski de fond	*fehr dew skee duh fawn*
cross-country skis	les skis de fond	*lay skee duh fawn*
cross the road	traverser	*trahvehrsay*
crossing	la traversée/ le croisement	*lah trahvehrsay/ luh krwahzmohn*
cry	pleurer	*pluhray*
cubic metre	le mètre cube	*luh mehtr kewb*
cucumber	le concombre	*luh kawnkawnbr*
cuddly toy	l'animal en peluche (m.)	*lahneemahl ohn plewsh*

cuff links	les boutons de manchette	*lay bootawn duh mohnsheht*
cup	la tasse	*lah tahs*
curly	frisé	*freezay*
current	la circulation	*lah seerkewlahsyawn*
cushion	le coussin	*luh koossahn*
customary	habituel	*ahbeetewehl*
customs	la douane	*lah dwahnn*
customs	le contrôle douanier	*luh kawntrol dwahnnyay*
cut (verb)	couper	*koopay*
cutlery	couverts	*koovehr*
cycling	faire de la bicyclette/du vélo	*fehr duh lah beeseekleht/ dew vayloa*

D

dairy produce	les produits laitiers	*lay prodwee laytyay*
damaged	abîmé	*ahbeemay*
dance	danser	*dohnsay*
dandruff	les pellicules	*lay payleekewl*
danger	le danger	*luh dohnjhay*
dangerous	dangereux	*dohnjhuhruh*
dark	sombre	*sawnbr*
date	le rendez-vous	*luh rohndayvoo*
daughter	la fille	*lah feey*
day	le jour	*luh jhoor*
day after tomorrow	après-demain	*ahpreh duhmahn*
day before yesterday	avant-hier	*ahvohn tyehr*
death	la mort	*lah mor*
decaffeinated	le décaféiné	*luh daykahfayeenay*
December	décembre	*daysohnbr*
deck chair	la chaise longue	*lah shehz lawng*
declare(customs)	déclarer	*dayklahray*
deep	profond	*profawn*
deep sea diving	la plongée sous-marine	*lah plawnjhay soo mahreen*
deepfreeze	le congélateur	*luh kawnjhaylahtuhr*
degrees	les degrés	*lay duhgray*

delay	le retard	*luh ruhtahr*
delicious	délicieux	*dayleesyuh*
dentist	le dentiste	*luh dohnteest*
dentures	le dentier	*luh dohntyay*
deodorant	le déodorant	*luh dayodorohn*
department	le rayon	*luh rayawn*
department store	le grand magasin	*luh grohn mahgahzahn*
departure	le départ	*luh daypahr*
departure time	l'heure de départ (f.)	*ler duh daypahr*
depilatory cream	la crème épilatoire	*lah krehm aypeelahtwahr*
deposit	arrhes, acompte	*ahr, ahkawnt*
dessert	le dessert	*luh dehssehr*
destination	la destination	*lah dehsteenahsyawn*
develop	développer	*dayvlopay*
diabetes	le diabète	*luh deeahbeht*
diabetic	le diabétique	*luh dyahbayteek*
dial	composer	*kawnpoazay*
diamond	le diamant	*luh deeahmohn*
diarrhoea	la diarrhée	*lah deeahray*
dictionary	le dictionnaire	*luh deeksyonehr*
diesel	le diesel	*luh dyayzehl*
diesel oil	le gas-oil	*luh gahzwahl*
diet	le régime	*luh rayjheem*
difficulty	la difficulté	*lah deefeekewltay*
digital	numérique	*newmehreek*
dining room	la salle à manger	*lah sahl ah mohnjhay*
dining/buffet car	le wagon-restaurant	*luh vahgawn rehstoaron*
dinner (to have)	dîner	*deenay*
dinner	le dîner	*luh deenay*
dinner jacket	le smoking	*luh smokeeng*
direction	la direction	*lah deerehksyawn*
directly	directement	*deerehktuhmohn*
dirty	sale	*sahl*
disabled	l'invalide (m./f.)	*lahnvahleed*
discount	la réduction	*lah raydewksyawn*
disgusting	dégoûtant	*daygootohn*

| dish | le plat | *luh plah* |

dish of the day	le plat du jour	*luh plah dew jhoor*
disinfectant	le désinfectant	*luh dayzahnfehktohn*
distance	la distance	*lah deestohns*
distilled water	l'eau distillée (f.)	*loa deesteelay*
disturb	déranger	*dayrohnjhay*
disturbance	troubles, tapage	*troobl, tapahjh*
dive	plonger	*plawnjhay*
diving	la plongée	*lah plawnjhay*
diving board	le plongeoir	*luh plawnjhwahr*
diving gear	l'équipement	*laykeepmohn*
	de plongeur (m.)	*duh plawnjhuhr*
DIY shop	le magasin	*luh mahgahzahn*
	de bricolage	*duh breekolajh*
dizzy	pris de vertige	*pree duh vehrteejh*
do (verb)	faire	*fehr*
doctor	le médecin	*luh maydsahn*
dog	le chien	*luh shyahn*
doll	la poupée	*lah poopay*
domestic	l'intérieur (m.) du pays	*lahntayryuhr dew pehy*
door	la porte	*lah port*
down	en bas	*ohn bah*
draught	le courant d'air	*luh koorohn dehr*
dream	rêver	*rehvay*
dress	la robe	*lah rob*
dressing gown	le peignoir	*luh paynywahr*
drink (verb)	boire	*bwahr*
drink	le verre	*luh vehr*
drinking chocolate	le chocolat au lait	*luh shoakoalah oa leh*
drinking water	l'eau potable (f.)	*loa potabl*
drive	conduire	*kawndweer*
driver	le chauffeur	*luh shoafuhr*
driving licence	le permis de	*luh pehrmee duh*
	conduire	*kawndweer*
drought	la sécheresse	*lah sayshrehs*
dry (verb)	sécher	*sayshay*
dry	sec	*sehk*
dry clean	nettoyer à sec	*nehtwahyay ah sehk*

dry cleaner's	la teinturerie	*lah tahntewruhree*
dry shampoo	le shampooing sec	*luh shohnpwahn sehk*
dummy	la tétine	*lah tayteen*
during	pendant	*pohndohn*
during the day	de jour	*duh jhoor*
DVD	DVD	*dayvayday*

E

each time	chaque fois	*shahk fwah*
ear	l'oreille (f.)	*lorehy*
ear, nose and throat specialist (ENT)	l'oto-rhino (m.)	*loatoa reenoa*
earache	le mal d'oreille	*luh mahl dorehy*
eardrops	les gouttes pour les oreilles	*lay goot poor lay zorehy*
early	tôt	*toa*
earrings	les boucles d'oreilles	*lay bookl dorehy*
earth	la terre	*lah tehr*
earthenware	la poterie	*lah potree*
east	l'est (m.)	*lehst*
easy	facile	*fahseel*
eat	manger	*mohnjhay*
eczema	l'eczéma (m.)	*lehgzaymah*
eel	l'anguille (f.)	*lohngeey*
egg	l'oeuf (m.)	*luhf*
elastic band	l'élastique (m.)	*laylahsteek*
electric	électrique	*aylehktreek*
electric current	le courant	*luh koorohn*
electricity	l'électricité (f.)	*laylehktreeseetay*
email	email / courier électronique	*eemehyl/cooreeay aylehktrohneek*
embassy	l'ambassade (f.)	*lohnbahsahd*
emergency brake	le frein de secours	*luh frahn duh suhkoor*
emergency exit	la sortie de secours	*lah sortee duh suhkoor*
emergency number	le numéro d'urgence (m.)	*luh newmayroa dewrzhohns*

emergency phone	le téléphone d'urgence (m.)	*luh taylayfon dewrjhohns*
emergency triangle	le triangle de signalisation	*luh treeohngl duh seenyahleezahsyawn*
emery board	la lime à ongles	*lah leem ah awngl*
empty	vide	*veed*
engaged	occupé	*okewpay*
England	Angleterre	*ohngluhtehr*
English	anglais	*ohngleh*
entertainment guide	le journal des spectacles	*luh jhoornal day spehktahkl*
envelope	l'enveloppe (f.)	*lohnvlop*
escort	l'hôtesse	*loatehs*
evening	le soir	*luh swahr*
evening wear	la tenue de soirée	*lah tuhnew duh swahray*
event	l'évènement (m.)	*layvehnmohn*
everything	tout	*too*
everywhere	partout	*pahrtoo*
examine	examiner	*ehgzahmeenay*
excavation	les fouilles	*lay fooeey*
excellent	excellent	*ehxaylohn*
exchange	échanger	*ayshohnjhay*
exchange office	le bureau de change	*luh bewroa duh shohnjh*
exchange rate	le cours du change	*luh koor dew shohnjh*
excursion	l'excursion (f.)	*lehxkewrsyawn*
exhibition	l'exposition (f.)	*lehxpoazeesyawn*
exit	la sortie	*lah sortee*
expenses	les frais	*lay freh*
expensive	cher	*shehr*
explain	expliquer	*ehxpleekay*
express	l'express (m.)	*lehxprehs*
external	extérieur	*ehxtayryuhr*
eye	l'oeil (m.)	*luhy*
eye drops	les gouttes pour les yeux	*lay goot poor lay zyuh*
eye shadow	le fard à paupières	*luh fahr ah poapyehr*
eye specialist	l'ophtalmologue (m.)	*loftahmolog*
eyeliner	l'eye-liner (m.)	*lahy leehnehr*

face	le visage	*luh veezajh*
factory	l'usine (f.)	*lewzeen*
fair	la foire	*lah fwahr*
fall	tomber	*tawnbay*
family	la famille	*lah fahmeey*
famous	célèbre	*saylehbr*
far away	éloigné	*aylwahnyay*
farm	la ferme	*lah fehrm*
farmer	le fermier	*luh fehrmyay*
fashion	la mode	*lah mod*
fast	rapidement	*rahpeedmohn*
father	le père	*luh pehr*
fault	la faute	*lah foat*
fax	faxer	*fahxay*
fear	la peur	*lah puhr*
February	février	*fayvryay*
feel	sentir	*sohnteer*
feel like	avoir envie (de)	*ahvwahr ohnvee (duh)*
fence	la clôture	*lah kloatewr*
fever	la fièvre	*lah feeyehvr*
fill (tooth)	plomber	*plawnbay*
fill out	remplir	*rohnpleer*
filling	le plombage	*luh plawnbahjh*
film	la pellicule	*lah payleekewl*
filter	le filtre	*luh feeltr*
filthy	crasseux	*krahssuh*
find	trouver	*troovay*
fine	la caution	*lah koasyawn*
fine (parking)	la contravention	*lah kawntrahvohnsyawn*
finger	le doigt	*luh dwah*
fire	le feu	*luh fuh*
fire brigade	les sapeurs pompiers	*lay sahpuhr pawnpyay*
fire escape	l'escalier de secours (m.)	*lehskahlyay duh suhkoor*
fire extinguisher	l'extincteur (m.)	*lehxtahntuhr*
first	le premier	*luh pruhmyay*

first aid	les premiers soins	lay pruhmyay swahn
first class	la première classe	lah pruhmyehr klahs
fish (verb)	pêcher	payshay
fish	le poisson	luh pwahssawn
fishing rod	la canne à pêche	lah kahnn ah pehsh
fitness centre	le centre de	luh sohntr duh
	mise en forme	meez ohn form
fitness training	l'entraînement de	lohntrehnmohn duh
	mise en forme (m.)	meez ohn form
fitting room	la cabine d'essayage	lah kahbeen dehsayahjh
fix	réparer	raypahray
flag	le drapeau	luh drahpoa
flash bulb	l'ampoule de flash (f.)	lohnpool duh flahsh
flash cube	le cube-flash	luh kewb flahsh
flash gun	le flash	luh flahsh
flat	l'appartement (m.)	lahpahrtuhmohn
flea market	le marché aux puces	luh mahrshay oa pews
flight	le vol	luh vol
flight number	le numéro de vol	luh newmayroa duh vol
flood	l'inondation (f.)	leenawndahsyawn
floor	l'étage (m.)	laytahjh
flour	la farine	lah fahreen
flu	la grippe	lah greep
fly-over	l'autopont (m.)	loatoapawn
fly (insect)	la mouche	lah moosh
fly (verb)	voler	volay
fog	le brouillard	luh brooy-yahr
foggy (to be)	faire du brouillard	fehr dew brooy-yahr
folding caravan	la caravane pliante	lah kahrahvahnn
		pleeohnt
follow	suivre	sweevr
food	la nourriture	lah nooreetewr
food poisoning	l'intoxication	lahntoxeekahsyawn
	alimentaire (f.)	ahleemohntehr
foodstuffs	les produits	lay prohdwee
	alimentaires	zahleemohntehr
foot	le pied	luh pyay

football (play)	jouer au football, le football	*jhooay oa footbol, luh footbol*
football match	le match de football	*luh mahch duh footbol*
for hire	à louer	*ah looay*
forbidden	interdit	*ahntehrdee*
forehead	le front	*luh frawn*
foreign	étranger	*aytrohnjhay*
forget	oublier	*oobleeay*
fork	la fourchette	*lah foorsheht*
form	le questionnaire	*luh kehstyonehr*
fort	le fort	*luh for*
fountain	la fontaine	*lah fawntehn*
frame	la monture	*lah mawntewr*
franc	le franc	*luh frohn*
free	libre	*leebr*
free of charge	gratuit	*grahtwee*
free time	les loisirs	*lay lwahzeer*
freeze	geler	*jhuhlay*
French	français	*frohnseh*
French (language)	le français	*luh frohnseh*
French bread	la baguette	*lah bahgeht*
fresh	frais	*freh*
Friday	vendredi	*vohndruhdee*
fried	frit	*free*
fried egg	l'oeuf sur le plat (m.)	*luhf sewr luh plah*
friend	l'ami(e) (m./f.)	*lahmee*
friendly	amical	*ahmeekahl*
fringe	la frange	*lah frohnjh*
fruit	le fruit	*luh frwee*
fruit juice	le jus de fruits	*luh jhew duh frwee*
frying pan	la poêle à frire	*lah pwahl ah freer*
full	plein	*plahn*
fun	le plaisir	*luh playzeer*
funny	drôle	*droal*

gallery	la galerie	*lah gahlree*
game	le jeu	*luh jhuh*
garage	le garage	*luh gahrahjh*
garbage bag	le sac poubelle	*luh sahk poobehl*
garden	le jardin	*luh jhahrdahn*
gastroenteritis	la gastro-entérite	*gahstroa ohntayreet*
gauze	la compresse de gaze	*lah kawnprehs duh gahz*
gel	le gel	*luh jhehl*
German	allemand	*ahlmohn*
get married	(se) marier	*(suh) mahryay*
get off	descendre	*daysohndr*
gift	le cadeau	*luh kahdoa*
gilt	doré	*doray*
ginger	le gingembre	*luh jhahnjhohnbr*
girl	la fille	*lah feey*
girlfriend	l'amie	*lahmee*
glacier	le glacier	*luh glahsyay*
glass (wine-)	le verre	*luh vehr*
glasses (sun-)	les lunettes	*lay lewneht*
glide	faire du vol à voile	*fehr dew vol ah vwahl*
glove	le gant	*luh gohn*
glue	la colle	*lah kol*
go	aller	*ahlay*
go back	reculer, retourner	*ruhkewlay, ruhtoornay*
go out	sortir	*sorteer*
goat's cheese	le fromage de chèvre	*luh fromajh duh shehvr*
gold	l'or (m.)	*lor*
golf course	le terrain de golf	*luh tehrahn duh golf*
good afternoon	bonjour	*bawnjhoor*
good evening	bonsoir	*bawnswahr*
good morning	bonjour	*bawnjhoor*
good night	bonne nuit	*bon nwee*
goodbye	au revoir	*oa ruhvwahr*
government	gouvernement	*goovehrnuhmohn*
gram	le gramme	*luh grahm*

grandchild	le petit enfant	*luh puhtee tohnfohn*
grandfather	le grand-père	*luh grohn pehr*
grandmother	la grand-mère	*lah grohn mehr*
grape juice	le jus de raisin	*luh jhew duh rayzahn*
grapefruit	le pamplemousse	*luh pohnpluhmoos*
grapes	les raisins	*lay rayzahn*
grass	l'herbe (f.)	*lehrb*
grave	la tombe	*lah townb*
greasy	gras	*grah*
green	vert	*vehr*
green card	la carte verte	*lah kahrt vehrt*
greet	saluer	*sahleway*
grey	gris	*gree*
grill	griller	*greeyay*
grilled	grillé	*greeyay*
grocer	l'épicier (m)	*laypeesyay*
ground	le sol	*luh sol*
group	le groupe	*luh groop*
guest house	la pension	*lah pohnsyawn*
guide (book)	le guide	*luh gueed*
guide (person)	le/la guide	*luh/lah gueed*
guided tour	la visite guidée	*lah veezeet gueeday*
gynaecologist	le gynécologue	*luh jheenaykolog*

H

hair	les cheveux	*lay shuhvuh*
hairbrush	la brosse à cheveux	*lah bros ah shuhvuh*
hairdresser	le coiffeur	*luh kwahfuhr*
hairdryer	sèche-cheveux	*sehsh shuhvuh*
hairslides	les barrettes	*lay bahreht*
hairspray	la laque	*lah lahk*
half (adj.)	demi	*duhmee*
half	la moitié	*lah mwahtyay*
half an hour	une demi-heure	*ewn demee uhr*
half full	à moitié plein	*ah mwahtyay plahn*
hammer	le marteau	*luh mahrtoa*

and	la main	*lah mahn*
and brake	le frein à main	*luh frahn ah mahn*
andbag	le sac à main	*luh sahk ah mahn*
andkerchief	le mouchoir	*luh mooshwahr*
andmade	fait-main	*feh mahn*
appy	heureux	*uhruh*
arbour	le port	*luh por*
ard	dur	*dewr*
at	le chapeau	*luh shahpoa*
ay fever	le rhume des foins	*luh rewm day fwahn*
azelnut	la noisette	*lah nwahzeht*
ead	la tête	*lah teht*
eadache	le mal de tête	*luh mahl duh teht*
eadscarf	le foulard	*luh foolahr*
ealth	la santé	*lah sohntay*
ealth food shop	le magasin diététique	*luh mahgahzahn dyaytayteek*
ear	entendre	*ohntohndr*
earing aid	la correction auditive	*lah korehksyawn oadeeteev*
eart	le coeur	*luh kuhr*
eater	le chauffage	*luh shoafahjh*
eavy	lourd	*loor*
eel	le talon	*luh tahlawn*
ello	bonjour, salut	*bawnjhoor, sahlew*
elmet	le casque	*luh kahsk*
elp (verb)	aider	*ayday*
elp	l'aide (f.)	*lehd*
erbal tea	l'infusion (f.)	*lahnfewzyawn*
ere	ici	*eesee*
erring	le hareng	*luh ahrohn*
igh	haut	*oa*
igh tide	le flux	*luh flew*
ighchair	la chaise d'enfant	*lah shehz dohnfohn*
iking	la marche à pied	*lah mahrsh ah pyay*
iking trip	la randonnée	*lah rohndonay*
ip	la hanche	*lah ohnsh*
ire	louer	*looay*

hitchhike	faire de l'auto-stop	*fehr duh loatoastop*
hobby	le passe-temps	*luh pahstohn*
hold-up	l'attaque (f.)	*lahtahk*
holiday house	la maison de vacances	*lah mehzawn duh vahkohns*
holidays	les vacances	*lay vahkohns*
homesickness	le mal du pays	*luh mahl dew pehy*
honest	honnête	*oneht*
honey	le miel	*luh myehl*
horizontal	horizontal	*oareezawntahl*
horrible	horrible	*oareebl*
horse	le cheval	*luh shuhvahl*
hospital	l'hôpital (m.)	*loapeetahl*
hospitality	l'hospitalité(f.)	*lospeetahleetay*
hot	chaud	*shoa*
hot-water bottle	la bouillotte	*lah booy-yot*
hot (spicy)	pimenté	*peemohntay*
hotel	l'hôtel (m.)	*loatehl*
hour	l'heure (f.)	*luhr*
house	la maison	*lah mehzawn*
household	les appareils	*lay zahpahrehy appliances*
houses of	le parlement	*luh pahrluhmohn parliament*
housewife	la femme au foyer	*lah fahm oa fwahyay*
how?	comment?	*komohn?*
how far?	c'est loin?	*seh lwahn?*
how long?	combien de temps?	*kawnbyahn duh tohn?*
how much?	combien?	*kawnbyahn?*
hungry (to be)	avoir faim	*ahvwahr fahn*
hurricane	l'ouragan (m.)	*loorahgohn*
hurry	la hâte	*lah aht*
husband	le mari	*luh mahree*
hut	la cabane	*lah kahbahnn*
hyperventilation	l'hyperventilation (f.)	*leepehrvohnteelahsyawn*

ice cream	la glace	*lah glahs*
ice cubes	les glaçons	*lay glahsawn*
ice skate	patiner	*pahteenay*
idea	l'idée (f.)	*leeday*
identification	la pièce d'identité	*lah pyehs deedohnteetay*
identify	identifier	*eedohnteefyay*
ignition key	la clef de contact	*lah klay duh kawntahkt*
ill	malade	*mahlahd*
illness	la maladie	*lah mahlahdee*
imagine	imaginer	*eemahjheenay*
immediately	immédiatement	*eemaydyahtmohn*
import duty	les droits de douane	*lay drwah duh dwahnn*
impossible	impossible	*ahnposeebl*
in	dans	*dohn*
in the evening	le soir	*luh swahr*
in the morning	le matin	*luh mahtahn*
included	compris	*kawnpree*
indicate	indiquer	*ahndeekay*
indicator	le clignotant	*luh kleenyotohn*
inexpensive	bon marché	*bawn mahrshay*
infection (viral/ bacterial)	l'infection (virale/ bactérielle) (f.)	*lahnfehksyawn (veerahl, bahktayryehl)*
inflammation	l'inflammation (f.)	*lahnflahmahsyawn*
information	l'information (f.)	*lahnformahsyawn*
information	le renseignement	*luh rohnsehnymohn*
information office	le bureau de renseignements	*luh bewroa duh rohnsehnymohn*
injection	la piqûre	*lah peekewr*
injured	blessé	*blehssay*
inner ear	l'oreille interne (f.)	*lorehy ahntehrn*
inner tube	la chambre à air	*lah shohnbr ah ehr*
innocent	innocent	*eenosohn*
insect	l'insecte (m.)	*lahnsehkt*
insect bite	la piqûre d'insecte	*lah peekewr dahnsehkt*

insect repellant	l'huile contre les moustiques	*lweel kawntr lay moosteek*
inside	à l'intérieur	*ah lahntayryuhr*
instructions	le mode d'emploi	*luh mod dohnplwah*
insurance	l'assurance (f.)	*lahsewrohns*
intermission	la pause	*lah poaz*
international	international	*ahntehrnahsyonahl*
interpreter	l'interprète (m./f.)	*lahntehrpreht*
intersection	le carrefour	*luh kahrfoor*
introduce oneself	se présenter	*suh prayzohntay*
invite	inviter	*ahnveetay*
invoice	la facture	*lah fahktewr*
iodine	l'iode (m.)	*lyod*
Ireland	l'Irlande (f.)	*leerlohnd*
Irish	irlandais	*leerlohndeh*
iron (verb)	repasser	*ruhpahsay*
iron	le fer à repasser	*luh fehr ah ruhpahsay*
ironing board	la table à repasser	*lah tahbl ah ruhpahsay*
island	l'île (f.)	*leel*
it's a pleasure	je vous en prie	*jhuh voo zohn pree*
Italian	italien	*eetahlyahn*
itch	la démangeaison	*lah daymohnjhehzawn*

J

jack	le cric	*luh kreek*
jacket	la veste	*lah vehst*
jam	la confiture	*lah kawnfeetewr*
January	janvier	*jhohnvyay*
jaw	la mâchoire	*lah mahshwahr*
jellyfish	la méduse	*lah maydewz*
jeweller	le bijoutier	*luh beejhootyay*
jewellery	les bijoux	*lay beejhoo*
jog	faire du jogging	*fehr dew jogeeng*
joke	la blague	*lah blahg*
juice	le jus	*luh jhew*
July	juillet	*jhweeyeh*

jump leads	le câble de démarrage	*luh kahbl duh daymahrahjh*
jumper	le pull-over	*luh pewlovehr*
June	juin	*jhwahn*

K

key	la clef/clé	*lah klay*
kilo	le kilo	*luh keeloa*
kilometre	le kilomètre	*luh keeloamehtr*
king	le roi	*luh rwah*
kiss (verb)	embrasser	*ohnbrahssay*
kiss	le baiser	*luh bayzay*
kitchen	la cuisine	*lah kweezeen*
knee	le genou	*luh jhuhnoo*
knee socks	les mi-bas	*lay mee bah*
knife	le couteau	*luh kootoa*
knit	tricoter	*treekotay*
know	savoir	*sahvwahr*

L

lace	la dentelle	*lah dohntehl*
ladies' toilets	les toilettes pour dames	*lay twahleht poor dahm*
lake	le lac	*luh lahk*
lamp	la lampe	*lah lohnp*
land	atterrir	*ahtayreer*
lane	la voie	*lah vwah*
language	la langue	*lah lohng*
laptop	ordinateur portable	*ohrdeenahtuhr pohrtahbl*
large	grand	*grohn*
last	dernier, passé	*dehrnyay, pahssay*
last night	la nuit passée	*lah nwee pahssay*
late	tard	*tahr*
later	tout à l'heure	*too tah luhr*
laugh	rire	*reer*
launderette	la laverie automatique	*lah lahvree oatoamahteek*

law	la loi	*lah lwah*
laxative	le laxatif	*luh lahxahteef*
leaky	crevé	*kruhvay*
leather	le cuir	*luh kweer*
leather goods	les articles de maroquinerie	*lay zahrteekl duh mahrokeenree*
leave	partir	*pahrteer*
leek	le poireau	*luh pwahroa*
left	gauche	*goash*
left luggage	la consigne	*lah kawnseeny*
left, on the	à gauche	*ah goash*
leg	la jambe	*lah jhohnb*
lemon	le citron	*luh seetrawn*
lemonade	la limonade	*lah leemonahd*
lend	prêter (à)	*prehtay (ah)*
lens	la lentille	*lah lohnteey*
lentils	les lentilles	*lay lohnteey*
less	moins	*mwahn*
lesson	la leçon	*lah luhsawn*
letter	la lettre	*lah lehtr*
lettuce	la laitue	*lah laytew*
level crossing	le passage à niveau	*luh pahssahjh ah neevoa*
library	la bibliothèque	*lah beebleeotehk*
lie (down)	s'étendre	*saytohndr*
lie (verb)	mentir	*mohnteer*
hitch-hiking	l'auto-stop	*loatoastop*
lift (in building)	l'ascenseur (m.)	*lahsohnsuhr*
lift (chair)	le télésiège	*luh taylaysyehjh*
light (not dark)	clair	*klehr*
light (not heavy)	léger	*layjhay*
light	la lumière	*lah lewmyehr*
lighter	le briquet	*luh breekeh*
lighthouse	le phare	*luh fahr*
lightning	la foudre	*lah foodr*
like	aimer	*aymay*
line	la ligne	*lah leenyuh*

linen	le lin	*luh lahn*
lipstick	le rouge à lèvres	*luh roohj ah lehvr*
liquorice	le réglisse	*luh rayglees*
listen	écouter	*aykootay*
literature	la littérature	*lah leetayrahtewr*
litre	le litre	*luh leetr*
little	peu	*puh*
live	habiter, vivre	*ahbeetay, veevr*
live together	habiter ensemble	*ahbeetay ohnsohnbl*
lobster	le homard	*luh omahr*
locally	localement	*lokahlmohn*
lock	la serrure	*lah sehrewr*
long	long	*lawn*
look	regarder	*ruhgahrday*
look for	chercher	*shehrshay*
look up	rechercher	*ruhshehrshay*
lorry	le camion	*luh kahmyawn*
lose	perdre	*pehrdr*
loss	la perte	*lah pehrt*
lost	introuvable, perdu	*ahntroovahbl, pehrdew*
lost item	l'objet perdu (m.)	*lohbjeh pehrdew*
lost property office	les objets trouvés	*lay zobjheh troovay*
lotion	la lotion	*lah loasyawn*
loud	fort	*for*
love (to be in)	être amoureux	*ehtr ahmooruh*
love (verb)	aimer	*aymay*
love	l'amour (m.)	*lahmoor*
low	bas	*bah*
low tide	le reflux	*luh ruhflew*
luck	la chance	*lah shohns*
luggage	le bagage	*luh bahgahjh*
luggage locker	la consigne automatique	*lah kawnseenyuh oatoamahteek*
lunch	le déjeuner	*luh dayjhuhnay*
lunchroom	le café	*luh kahfay*
lungs	les poumons	*lay poomawn*

macaroni	les macaronis	*lay mahkahroanee*
madam	madame	*mahdahm*
magazine	la revue	*lah ruhvew*
mail	le courrier	*luh kooryay*
main post office	le bureau de poste central	*luh bewroa duh post sohntral*
main road	la grande route	*lah grohnd root*
make an appointment	prendre un rendez-vous	*prohndr uhn rohndayvoo*
make love	faire l'amour	*fehr lahmoor*
makeshift	provisoirement	*proveezwahrmohn*
man	l'homme (m.)	*lom*
manager	le directeur	*luh deerehktuhr*
manicure	la manucure	*lah mahnewkewr*
map	la carte géographique	*lah kahrt jhayoagrahfeek*
marble	le marbre	*luh mahrbruh*
March	mars	*mahrs*
marina	le port de plaisance	*luh por duh playzohns*
market	le marché	*luh mahrshay*
marriage	le mariage	*luh mahryajh*
married	marié	*mahreeay*
mass	la messe	*lah mehs*
massage	le massage	*luh mahsahjh*
mat	mat	*maht*
match	le match	*luh mahch*
matches	les allumettes	*lay zahlewmeht*
May	mai	*meh*
maybe	peut-être	*puh tehtr*
mayonnaise	la mayonnaise	*lah mahyonehz*
mayor	le maire	*luh mehr*
meal	le repas	*luh ruhpah*
mean	signifier	*seenyeefyay*
meat	la viande	*lah vyohnd*
medical insurance	l'assurance maladie (f.)	*lahsewrohns mahlahdee*
medication	le médicament	*luh maydeekahmohn*

medicine	le médicament	*luh maydeekahmohn*
meet	rencontrer	*rohnkohntray*
melon	le melon	*luh muhlawn*
membership	l'adhésion (f.)	*lahdayzyawn*
menstruate	avoir ses règles	*ahvwahr say rehgl*
menstruation	les règles	*lay rehgl*
menu	la carte	*lah kahrt*
menu of the day	le menu du jour	*luh muhnew dew jhoor*
message	le message	*luh mehsahjh*
metal	le métal	*luh maytahl*
meter	le compteur	*luh kawntuhr*
metre	le mètre	*luh mehtr*
migraine	la migraine	*lah meegrehn*
mild (tobacco)	léger	*layjhay*
milk	le lait	*luh leh*
millimetre	le millimètre	*luh meeleemehtr*
milometer	le compteur kilométrique	*luh kawntuhr keeloamaytreek*
mince	la viande hachée	*lah vyohnd ahshay*
mineral water	l'eau minérale (f.)	*loa meenayral*
minute	la minute	*lah meenewt*
mirror	le miroir	*luh meerwahr*
miss	manquer	*mohnkay*
missing (to be)	manquer	*mohnkay*
mistake	l'erreur (f.)	*lehruhr*
misunderstanding	le malentendu	*luh mahlohntohndew*
mocha	le moka	*luh mokah*
modern art	l'art moderne (m.)	*lahr modehrn*
molar	la molaire	*lah molehr*
moment	le moment	*luh momohn*
Monday	lundi	*luhndee*
money	l'argent (m.)	*lahrjhohn*
month	le mois	*luh mwah*
moped	le cyclomoteur	*luh seekloamotuhr*
morning-after pill	la pilule du lendemain	*lah peelewl dew lohnduhmahn*
mosque	la mosquée	*lah moskay*

motel	le motel	luh moatehl
mother	la mère	lah mehr
moto-cross	le moto-cross	luh moatoakros
motorbike	la motocyclette	lah moatoaseekleht
motorboat	le bateau à moteur	luh bahtoa ah motuhr
motorway	l'autoroute (f.)	loatoaroot
mountain	la montagne	lah mawntanyuh
mountain hut	le refuge	luh ruhfewjh
mountaineering	l'alpinisme (m.)	lahlpeeneesm
mountaineering shoes	les chaussures de montagne	lay shoasewr duh mawntanyuh
mouse	la souris	lah sooree
mouth	la bouche	lah boosh
much/many	beaucoup	boakoo
multi-storey car park	le parking	luh pahrkeeng
muscle	le muscle	luh mewskl
muscle spasms	les crampes musculaires	lay krohnp mewskewlehr
museum	le musée	luh mewzay
mushrooms	les champignons	lay shohnpeenyawn
music	la musique	lah mewzeek
musical	la comédie musicale	lah komaydee mewzeekahl
mussels	les moules	lay mool
mustard	la moutarde	lah mootahrd

N

nail	le clou	luh kloo
nail (on hand)	l'ongle (m.)	lawngl
nail polish	le vernis à ongles	luh vehrnee ah awngl
nail polish remover	le dissolvant	luh deesolvohn
nail scissors	le coupe-ongles	luh koop awngl
naked	nu	new
nappy	la couche	lah koosh
nationality	la nationalité	lah nahsyonahleetay
natural	naturel	nahtewrehl
nature	la nature	lah nahtewr

naturism	le naturisme (m.)	*luh nahtewreesm*
nauseous	(avoir) mal au coeur	*(ahvwahr) mahl oa kuhr*
near	près	*preh*
nearby	tout près	*too preh*
necessary	nécessaire	*naysehsehr*
neck	le collier	*luh kolyay*
necklace	la chaîne	*lah shehn*
nectarine	la nectarine	*lah nehktahreen*
needle	l'aiguille (f.)	*laygweey*
neighbours	les voisins	*lay vwahzahn*
nephew	le neveu	*luh nuhvuh*
Netherlands	les Pays-Bas	*lay pehy bah*
never	jamais	*jhahmeh*
new	nouveau	*noovoa*
news	les informations	*lay zahnformahsyawn*
news stand	le kiosque	*luh kyosk*
newspaper	le journal	*luh jhoornahl*
next	le prochain	*luh proshahn*
next to	à côté de	*ah koatay duh*
nice	agréable, bon	*ahgrayahbl, bawn*
nice (friendly)	gentil	*jhohntee*
niece	la nièce	*lah nyehs*
night	la nuit	*lah nwee*
night duty	le service de nuit	*luh sehrvees duh nwee*
nightclub	la boîte de nuit/ le night-club	*lah bwaht duh nwee/ luh naheet kluhb*
nightlife	la vie nocturne	*lah vee noktewrn*
nipple	la tétine	*lah tayteen*
no	non	*nawn*
no overtaking	l'interdiction de dépasser (f.)	*lahntehrdeeksyawn duh daypahsay*
no-one	personne	*pehrson*
noise	le bruit	*luh brwee*
nonstop	continu	*kawnteenew*
normal	normal, ordinaire	*normahl, ordeenehr*
north	le nord	*luh nor*
nose	le nez	*luh nay*

nose bleed	le saignement de nez	*luh sehnyuhmohn dew nay*
nose drops	les gouttes pour le nez	*lay goot poor luh nay*
notepaper	le papier postal	*luh pahpyay postahl*
nothing	rien	*ryahn*
November	novembre	*novohnbr*
nowhere	nulle part	*newl pahr*
nudist beach	la plage de nudistes	*lah plahjh duh newdeest*
number	le numéro	*luh newmayroa*
number plate	la plaque d'immatriculation	*lah plahk deemahtree-kewlahsyawn*
nurse	l'infirmière (f.)	*lahnfeermyehr*
nutmeg	la noix de muscade	*lah nwah duh mewskahd*
nuts	les noix	*lay nwah*

O

October	octobre	*oktobr*
off licence	le marchand de vin	*luh mahrshohn duh vahn*
offer	offrir	*ofreer*
office	le bureau	*luh bewroa*
oil	l'huile (f.)	*lweel*
oil level	le niveau d'huile	*luh neevoa dweel*
ointment	le baume	*luh boam*
ointment for burns	la pommade contre les brûlures	*lah pomahd kawntr lay brewlewr*
okay	d'accord	*dahkor*
old	vieux	*vyuh*
old town	la vieille ville	*lah vyehy veel*
olive oil	l'huile d'olive	*lweel doleev*
olives	les olives	*lay zoleev*
omelette	l'omelette (f.)	*lomleht*
on	sur	*sewr*
on board	à bord	*ah bor*
on the way	en cours de route	*ohn koor duh root*
oncoming car	le véhicule en sens inverse	*luh vayeekewl ohn sohns ahnvehr*

one-way traffic	la circulation à sens unique	*lah seerkewlahsyawn ah sohns ewneek*
one hundred grams	cent grammes	*sohn grahm*
onion	l'oignon (m.)	*lonyawn*
open (verb)	ouvrir	*oovreer*
open	ouvert	*oovehr*
opera	l'opéra (m.)	*loapayrah*
operate	opérer	*oapayray*
operator (telephone)	la téléphoniste	*lah taylayfoneest*
operetta	l'opérette (f.)	*loapayreht*
opposite	en face	*ohn fahs*
optician	l'opticien (m.)	*lopteesyahn*
or	ou	*oo*
orange	l'orange (f.)	*lorohnjh*
orange (adj.)	orange	*orohnjh*
orange juice	le jus d'orange	*luh jhew dorohnjh*
order (verb)	commander	*komohnday*
order	la commande	*lah kohmohnd*
other	l'autre	*loatr*
other side	l'autre côté	*loatr koatay*
outside	dehors	*duh-or*
overtake	doubler	*dooblay*
oysters	les huîtres	*lay zweetr*

P

package (post)	le paquet postal	*luh pahkeh postahl*
packed lunch	le casse-croûte	*luh kahs kroot*
page	la page	*lah pahjh*
pain	la douleur	*lah dooluhr*
painkiller	le calmant	*luh kahlmohn*
paint	la peinture	*lah pahntewr*
painting (art)	le tableau	*luh tahbloa*
palace	le palais	*luh pahleh*
pan	la casserole	*lah kahsrol*
pancake	la crèpe	*lah krehp*
pane	la vitre	*lah veetr*

pants	la culotte	*lah kewlot*
panty liner	le protège-slip	*luh protehjh sleep*
paper	le papier	*luh pahpyay*
paraffin oil	le pétrole	*luh paytrol*
parasol	le parasol	*luh pahrahsol*
parcel	le colis	*luh kolee*
pardon	pardon	*pahrdawn*
parents	les parents	*lay pahrohn*
park	le parc	*luh pahrk*
park (verb)	garer	*gahray*
parking space	la place de parking	*lah plahs duh pahrkeeng*
parsley	le persil	*luh pehrsee*
part	la pièce	*lah pyehs*
partition	la séparation	*lah saypahrahsyawn*
partner	le/la partenaire	*luh/lah pahrtuhnehr*
party	la fête	*lah feht*
passable	praticable	*prahteekahbl*
passenger	le passager	*luh pahsahjhay*
passport	le passeport	*luh pahspor*
passport photo	la photo d'identité	*lah foatoa deedohnteetay*
patient	le patient	*luh pahsyohn*
pavement	le trottoir	*luh trotwahr*
pay	payer	*payay*
peach	la pêche	*lah pehsh*
peanuts	les cacahuètes	*lay kahkahweht*
pear	la poire	*lah pwahr*
peas	les petits pois	*lay puhtee pwah*
pedal	la pédale	*lah paydahl*
pedestrian crossing	le passage clouté	*luh pahsahjh klootay*
pedicure	le/la pédicure	*luh/lah paydeekewr*
pen	le stylo	*luh steeloa*
pencil	le crayon	*luh krayawn*
penis	le pénis	*luh paynees*
pepper (capsicum)	le poivron	*luh pwahvrawn*
pepper	le poivre	*luh pwahvr*
performance	la représentation	*lah ruhprayzohntahsyawn*
	de théâtre	*duh tayahtr*

perfume	le parfum	*luh pahrfuhn*
perm (verb)	faire une permanente à	*fehr ewn pehrmahnohnt ah*
perm	la permanente	*lah pehrmahnohnt*
permit	le permis	*luh pehrmee*
person	la personne	*lah pehrson*
personal	personnel	*pehrsonehl*
petrol	l'essence (f.)	*lehssohns*
petrol station	la station-service	*lah stahsyawn sehrvees*
pets	les animaux domestiques	*lay zahneemoa domehsteek*
pharmacy	la pharmacie	*lah fahrmahsee*
phone (tele-)	le téléphone	*luh taylayfon*
phone (verb)	téléphoner	*taylayfonay*
phone box	la cabine téléphonique	*lah kahbeen taylayfoneek*
phone charger	chargeur de téléphone	*shahrjhuhr duh taylayfohn*
phone directory	l'annuaire	*lahnnewehr*
phone number	le numéro de téléphone	*luh newmayroa duh taylayfon*
photo	la photo	*la foatoa*
photocopier	le photocopieur	*luh foatoakopyuhr*
photocopy (verb)	photocopier	*foatoakopyay*
photocopy	la photocopie	*lah foatoakopee*
pick up	aller chercher	*ahlay shehrshay*
picnic	le pique-nique	*luh peek neek*
pier	la jetée	*lah jhuhtay*
pigeon	le pigeon	*luh peejhyawn*
pill (contraceptive)	la pilule	*lah peelewl*
pillow	le coussin	*luh koossahn*
pillowcase	la taie d'oreiller	*lah tay dorehyay*
pin	l'épingle (f.)	*laypahngl*
pineapple	l'ananas (m.)	*lahnahnahs*
pipe	la pipe	*lah peep*
pipe tobacco	le tabac à pipe	*luh tahbah ah peep*
pity	dommage	*domahjh*
places of entertainment	les possibilités de sortie	*lay poseebeeleetay duh sortee*
places of interest	les curiosités	*lay kewryozeetay*

plan	l'intention (f.)	*lahntohnsyawn*
plant	la plante	*lah plohnt*
plaster	le sparadrap	*luh spahrahdrah*
plastic	plastique	*plahsteek*
plastic bag	le sac en plastique	*luh sahk ohn plahsteek*
plate	l'assiette (f.)	*lahsyeht*
platform	la voie, le quai	*lah vwah, luh kay*
play (theatre)	la pièce de théâtre	*lah pyehs duh tayahtr*
play (verb)	jouer	*jhooay*
play basketball	jouer au basket	*jhooay oa bahskeht*
play billiards	jouer au billiard	*jhooay oa biy-yahr*
play chess	jouer aux échecs	*jhooay oa zayshehk*
play draughts	jouer aux dames	*jhooay oa dahm*
play golf	jouer au golf	*jhooay oa golf*
playing cards	les cartes à jouer	*lay kahrt ah jhooay*
pleasant	agréable	*ahgrayahbl*
please	s'il vous plaît	*seel voo pleh*
pleasure	la satisfaction	*lah sahteesfahksyawn*
plum	la prune	*lah prewn*
pocketknife	le canif	*luh kahneef*
point	indiquer	*ahndeekay*
poison	le poison	*luh pwahzawn*
police	la police	*lah polees*
police station	le poste de police	*luh post duh polees*
policeman	l'agent de police (m.)	*lahjhohn duh polees*
pond	le bassin	*luh bahsahn*
pony	le poney	*luh poaneh*
pop concert	le concert pop	*luh kawnsehr pop*
population	la population	*lah popewlahsyawn*
pork	la viande de porc	*lah vyohnd duh por*
port	le porto	*luh portoa*
porter	le porteur	*luh portuhr*
post code	le code postal	*luh kod postahl*
post office	la poste	*lah post*
postage	le port	*luh por*
postbox	la boîte aux lettres	*lah bwaht oa lehtr*

postcard	la carte postale	*lah kahrt postahl*
postman	le facteur	*luh fahktuhr*
potato	la pomme de terre	*lah pom duh tehr*
poultry	la volaille	*lah vohlahy*
pound	la livre	*lah leevr*
powdered milk	le lait en poudre	*luh leh ohn poodr*
prawns	les crevettes roses	*lay kruhveht roaz*
precious	précieux	*praysyuh*
prefer	préférer	*prayfayray*
preference	la préférence	*lah prayfayrohns*
pregnant	enceinte	*ohnsahnt*
present (adj.)	présent	*prayzohn*
present	le cadeau	*luh kahdoa*
press	appuyer	*ahpweeyay*
pressure	la pression	*lah prehsyawn*
price	le prix	*luh pree*
price list	la liste de prix	*lah leest duh pree*
print (verb)	faire tirer	*fehr teeray*
print	l'épreuve (f.)	*laypruhv*
probably	probablement	*probahbluhmohn*
problem	le problème	*luh problehm*
profession	la profession	*lah profehsyawn*
programme	le programme	*luh prograhm*
pronounce	prononcer	*proanawnsay*
propane gas	le gaz propane	*luh gahz propahn*
pull	arracher	*ahrahshay*
pull a muscle	froisser un muscle	*frwahsay uhn mewskl*
pure	pur	*pewr*
purple	violet	*veeoleh*
purse	le porte-monnaie	*luh port moneh*
push	pousser	*poossay*
pushchair	la poussette	*lah poosseht*
puzzle	le puzzle	*luh puhzl*
pyjamas	le pyjama	*luh peejhahmah*

Q

quarter	le quart	*luh kahr*
quarter of an hour	le quart d'heure	*luh kahr duhr*
queen	la reine	*lah rehn*
question	la question	*lah kehstyawn*
quick	rapide	*rahpeed*
quiet	tranquille	*trohnkeey*

R

radio	la radio	*lah rahdyoa*
railways	les chemins de fer (m.)	*lay shuhmahn duh fehr*
rain (verb)	pleuvoir	*pluhvwahr*
rain	la pluie	*lah plwee*
raincoat	l'imperméable (m.)	*lahnpehrmayahbl*
raisins	les raisins secs	*lay rehzahn sehk*
rape	le viol	*luh vyol*
rapids	le courant rapide	*luh koorohn rahpeed*
raspberries	les framboises	*lay frohnbwahz*
raw	cru	*krew*
raw ham	le jambon cru	*luh jhohnbawn krew*
raw vegetables	les crudités	*lay krewdeetay*
razor blades	les lames de rasoir	*lay lahm duh rahzwahr*
read (verb)	lire	*leer*
ready	prêt	*preh*
really	vraiment	*vrehmohn*
receipt (till)	le ticket de caisse	*luh teekeh duh kehs*
receipt	le reçu, la quittance	*luh ruhsew, lah keetohns*
recipe	la recette	*lah ruhseht*
reclining chair	la chaise longue	*lah shehz lawng*
recommend	recommander	*ruhkomohnday*
recovery service	l'assistance routière (f.)	*lahseestohns rootyehr*
rectangle	le rectangle	*luh rehktohngl*
red	rouge	*roojh*
red wine	le vin rouge	*luh vahn roojh*
reduction	la réduction	*lah raydewksyawn*

refrigerator	le réfrigérateur	*luh rayfreejhayrahtuhr*
regards	les amitiés	*lay zahmeetyay*
region	la région	*lah rayjhyawn*
registration	la carte grise	*lah kahrt greez*
relatives	la famille	*lah fahmeey*
reliable	sûr	*sewr*
religion	la religion	*lah ruhleejhyawn*
rent out	louer	*looay*
repair (verb)	réparer	*raypahray*
repairs	la réparation	*lah raypahrahsyawn*
repeat	répéter	*raypaytay*
report	le procès-verbal	*luh proseh vehrbahl*
resent	prendre mal	*prohndr mahl*
responsible	responsable	*rehspawnsahbl*
rest	se reposer	*suh ruhpoazay*
restaurant	le restaurant	*luh rehstoarohn*
result	le résultat	*luh rayzewltah*
retired	à la retraite	*ah lah ruhtreht*
retirement	la retraite	*lah ruhtreht*
return (ticket)	l'aller-retour (m.)	*lahlay ruhtoor*
reverse (vehicle)	faire marche arrière	*fehr mahrsh ahryehr*
rheumatism	le rhumatisme	*luh rewmahteesm*
rice	le riz	*luh ree*
ridiculous	ridicule	*reedeekewl*
riding (horseback)	faire du cheval	*fehr dew shuhvahl*
riding school	le manège	*luh mahnehjh*
right	la droite	*lah drwaht*
right, on the	à droite	*ah drwaht*
right of way	la priorité	*lah preeoreetay*
ripe	mûr	*mewr*
risk	le risque	*luh reesk*
river	la rivière	*reevyehr*
road	la route	*lah root*
roasted	rôti	*roatee*
rock	le rocher	*luh roshay*
roll	le petit pain	*luh puhtee pahn*
rolling tobacco	le tabac à rouler	*luh tahbah ah roolay*

roof rack	la galerie	*lah gahlree*
room	la pièce	*lah pyehs*
room number	le numéro de chambre	*luh newmayroa duh shohnbr*
room service	le service de chambre	*luh sehrvees duh shohnbr*
rope	la corde	*lah kord*
rose	la rose	*lah roaz*
rosé	le rosé	*luh roazay*
roundabout	le rond-point	*luh rawn pwahn*
route	l'itinéraire (m.)	*leeteenayrehr*
rowing boat	la barque	*la bahrk*
rubber	le caoutchouc	*luh kah-oochoo*
rubbish	les détritus	*luh daytreetews*
rucksack	le sac à dos	*luh sahk ah doa*
rude	mal élevé	*mahl aylvay*
ruins	les ruines (f.)	*lay rween*
run into	rencontrer	*rohnkawntray*
running shoes	les chaussures de sport	*lay shoasewr duh spor*

S

sad	triste	*treest*
safari	le safari	*luh sahfahree*
safe (adj.)	en sécurité	*ohn saykewreetay*
safe	le coffre-fort	*luh kofr for*
safety pin	l'épingle de nourrice (f.)	*laypahngl duh noorees*
sail	faire de la voile	*fehr duh lah vwahl*
sailing boat	le voilier	*luh vwahlyay*
salad	la salade	*lah sahlahd*
salad oil	l'huile de table (f.)	*lweel duh tahbl*
salami	le salami	*luh sahlahmee*
sale	les soldes	*lay sold*
salt	le sel	*luh sehl*
same	le même	*luh mehm*
sandwich	le sandwich	*luh sohndweech*
sandy beach	la plage de sable	*lah plahjh duh sahbl*
sanitary towel	la serviette hygiénique	*lah sehrvyeht eejhyayneek*

sardines	les sardines	lay sahrdeen
satellite TV	télé par satellite	taylay pahr sahtehleet
satisfied	content (de)	kawntohn (duh)
Saturday	samedi	sahmdee
sauce	la sauce	lah soas
sauna	le sauna	luh soanah
sausage	la saucisse	lah soasees
savoury	salé	sahlay
say	dire	deer
scarf	l'écharpe (f.)	layshahrp
scenic walk	le circuit pédestre	luh seerkwee paydehstr
school	l'école (f.)	laykol
scissors	les ciseaux	lay seezoa
scooter	le scooter	luh skootehr
scorpion	le scorpion	luh skorpyawn
Scotland	l'Ecosse (f.)	laykos
Scottish	écossais	aykosseh
scrambled eggs	l'oeuf brouillé (m.)	lef brooy-yay
screw	la vis	lah vees
screwdriver	le tournevis	luh toornuhvees
sculpture	la sculpture	lah skewltewr
sea	la mer	lah mehr
seasick (to be)	avoir le mal de mer	ahvwahr luh mahl duh mehr
seat	la place	lah plahs
second-hand	d'occasion	dokahzyawn
second (adj.)	deuxième	duhzyehm
second	la seconde	lah suhgawnd
sedative	le tranquillisant	luh trohnkeeleezohn
self-timer	le déclencheur automatique	luh dayklohnshuhr oatoamahteek
semi-skimmed	demi-écrémé	duhmee aykraymay
send	expédier	ehxpaydyay
sentence	la phrase	lah frahz
separated	séparé	saypahray
September	septembre	sehptohnbr
serious	sérieux	sayryuh

service	le service	*luh sehrvees*
serviette	la serviette	*lah sehrvyeht*
set (hair)	faire une mise en plis	*fehr ewn meez ohn plee*
sewing thread	le fil à coudre	*luh feel ah koodr*
shade	l'ombre (f.)	*lawnbr*
shallow	peu profond	*puh profawn*
shampoo	le shampooing	*luh shohnpwahn*
shark	le requin	*luh ruhkahn*
shave (verb)	se raser	*suh rahzay*
shaver	le rasoir électrique	*luh rahzwahr aylehktreek*
shaving brush	le blaireau	*luh blayroa*
shaving cream	la crème à raser	*lah krehm ah rahzay*
shaving soap	le savon à raser	*luh sahvawn ah rahzay*
sheet	le drap	*luh drah*
sherry	le xérès	*luh ksayrehz*
shirt	la chemise	*lah shuhmeez*
shoe	la chaussure	*lah shoasewr*
shoe polish	le cirage	*luh seerajh*
shoe shop	le magasin de chaussures	*luh mahgahzahn duh shoasewr*
shoelace	le lacet	*luh lahseh*
shoemaker	le cordonnier	*luh kordonyay*
shop (verb)	faire les courses	*fehr lay koors*
shop	le magasin	*luh mahgahzahn*
shop assistant	la vendeuse	*lah vohnduhz*
shop window	la vitrine	*lah veetreen*
shopping bag	le cabas	*luh kahbah*
shopping centre	le centre commercial	*luh sohntr komehrsyahl*
short	court	*koor*
short circuit	le court-circuit	*luh koor seerkwee*
shorts	le bermuda	*luh behrmewdah*
shoulder	l'épaule (f.)	*laypoal*
show	le spectacle	*luh spehktahkl*
shower	la douche	*lah doosh*
shutter	l'obturateur (m.)	*lobtewrahtuhr*
sieve	la passoire	*lah pahswahr*
sign (verb)	signer	*seenyay*

sign	le panneau	*luh pahnoa*
signature	la signature	*lah seenyahtewr*
silence	le silence	*luh seelohns*
silver	l'argent (m.)	*lahrjhohn*
silver-plated	argenté	*ahrjhohntay*
simple	simple	*sahnpl*
single (ticket)	l'aller simple (m.)	*lahlay sahnpl*
single (unmarried)	célibataire	*sayleebahtehr*
single	le célibataire	*luh sayleebahtehr*
sir	monsieur	*muhsyuh*
sister	la soeur	*lah suhr*
sit (verb)	s'asseoir	*sahswahr*
size	la pointure, la taille	*lah pwahntewr, lah tahy*
ski (verb)	skier, faire du ski	*skeeay, fehr dew skee*
ski boots	les chaussures de ski	*lay shoasewr duh skee*
ski goggles	les lunettes de ski	*lay lewneht duh skee*
ski instructor	le moniteur de ski	*luh moneetuhr duh skee*
ski lessons/class	le cours de ski, la classe de ski	*luh koor duh skee, lah klahs duh skee*
ski lift	le remonte-pente	*luh ruhmawnt pohnt*
ski pants	le pantalon de ski	*luh pohntahlawn duh skee*
ski pass	le forfait de ski	*luh forfeh duh skee*
ski slope	la piste de ski	*lah peest duh skee*
ski stick	le bâton de ski	*luh bahtawn duh skee*
ski suit	la combinaison de ski	*lah kawnbeeneh- zawn duh skee*
ski wax	le fart à ski	*luh fahr ah skee*
skimmed	écrémé	*aykraymay*
skin	la peau	*lah poa*
skirt	la jupe	*lah jhewp*
skis	les skis	*lay skee*
sledge	la luge	*lah lewjh*
sleep (verb)	dormir	*dormeer*
sleep well	dormez-bien	*dormay byahn*
sleeping car	le wagon-lit	*luh vahgawn lee*
sleeping pills	les somnifères	*lay somneefehr*
slim	mince	*mahns*

slip	la combinaison	lah kawnbeenehzawn
slip road	la bretelle d'accès	lah bruhtehl dahkseh
slow	lentement	lohntuhmohn
small	petit	puhtee
small change	la monnaie	lah moneh
smell (verb)	puer	peway
smoke	la fumée	lah fewmay
smoke (verb)	fumer	fewmay
smoked	fumé	fewmay
smoking compartment	le compartiment fumeurs	luh kawnpahrteemohn fewmuhr
snake	le serpent	luh sehrpohn
snorkel	le tuba	luh tewbah
snow (verb)	neiger	nehjhay
snow	la neige	lah nehjh
snow chains	les chaînes	lay shehn
soap	le savon	luh sahvawn
soap box	la boîte à savon	lah bwaht ah sahvawn
socket	la prise	lah preez
socks	les chaussettes	lay shoasseht
soft drink	la boisson fraîche	lah bwahssawn frehsh
sole (fish)	la sole	lah sol
sole (shoe)	la semelle	lah suhmehl
solicitor	l'avocat	lahvoakah
someone	quelqu'un	kehlkuhn
something	quelque chose	kehlkuhshoaz
sometimes	parfois	pahrfwah
somewhere	quelque part	kehlkuhpahr
son	le fils	luh fees
soon	bientôt	byahntoa
sorbet	le sorbet	luh sorbeh
sore (be)	faire mal	fehr mal
sore throat	le mal de gorge	luh mahl duh gorjh
sorry	pardon	pahrdawn
sort	la sorte	lah sort
soup	la soupe	lah soop
sour	acide	ahseed

sour cream	la crème fraîche	*lah krehm frehsh*
source	la source	*lah soors*
south	le sud	*luh sewd*
souvenir	le souvenir	*luh soovneer*
spaghetti	les spaghetti	*lay spahgehtee*
spanner (open-ended)	las clé plate	*lay klay plaht*
spanner	la clef à molette	*lah klay ah moleht*
spare parts	les pièces détachées	*lay pyehs daytashay*
spare tyre	le pneu de rechange	*luh pnuh duh ruhshohnjh*
spare wheel	la roue de secours	*lah roo duh suhkoor*
speak (verb)	parler	*pahrlay*
special	spécial	*spaysyahl*
specialist	le spécialiste	*luh spaysyahleest*
specialty	la spécialité	*lah spaysyahleetay*
speed limit	la vitesse maximum	*lah veetehs mahxeemuhm*
spell (verb)	épeler	*aypuhlay*
spices	les épices	*lay zaypees*
spicy	épicé	*aypeesay*
splinter	l'écharde (f.)	*layshahrd*
spoon	la cuillère	*lah kweeyehr*
spoonful	la cuillerée	*lah kweeyuhray*
sport	le sport	*luh spor*
sports centre	la salle de sport	*lah sahl duh spohr*
spot (place)	l'endroit (m.)	*lohndrwah*
sprain	fouler	*foolay*
spring	le printemps	*luh prahntoh*
square	le carré	*luh kahray*
square (town)	la place	*lah plahs*
square metre	le mètre carré	*luh mehtr kahray*
squash	le squash	*luh skwahsh*
stadium	le stade	*luh stahd*
stain	la tache	*lah tahsh*
stain remover	le détachant	*luh daytahshoh*
stairs	l'escalier (m.)	*lehskahlyay*
stalls	la salle	*lah sahl*
stamp	le timbre	*luh tahnbr*
start (verb)	démarrer	*daymahray*

station	la gare	*lah gahr*
statue	la statue	*lah stahtew*
stay (lodge)	loger	*lohjhay*
stay (remain)	rester	*rehstay*
stay	le séjour	*luh sayjhoor*
steal	voler	*volay*
steel	acier	*ahsyay*
stench	la mauvaise odeur	*lah moavehz oduhr*
sting	piquer	*peekay*
stitch (med.)	la suture	*lah sewtewr*
stitch (verb)	suturer	*sewtewray*
stock	le consommé	*luh kawnsomay*
stockings	les bas	*lay bah*
stomach	l'estomac (m.)/ le ventre	*lehstomah/luh vohntr*
stomach ache	mal au ventre/ le mal d'estomac	*mahl oa vohntr/ luh mahl dehstomah*
stomach cramps	les spasmes abdominaux	*lay spahzm zahbdomeenoa*
stools (med.)	les selles	*lay sehl*
stop (verb)	arrêter	*ahrehtay*
stop	l'arrêt (m.)	*lahreh*
stopover	l'escale (f.)	*lehskahl*
storm	la tempête	*lah tohnpeht*
straight	raide	*rehd*
straight ahead	tout droit	*too drwah*
straw	la paille	*lah pahy*
street	la rue	*lah rew*
street (side)	côté rue	*koatay rew*
strike	la grève	*lah grehv*
study	faire des études	*fehr day zaytewd*
subscriber's number	le numéro d'abonné	*luh newmayroa dahbonay*
subtitled	sous-titré	*soo teetray*
succeed	réussir	*rayewsseer*
sugar	le sucre	*luh sewkr*
sugar lumps	les morceaux de sucre	*lay morsoa duh sewkr*
suit	le costume	*luh kostewm*

suitcase	la valise	*lah vahleez*
summer	l'été (m.)	*laytay*
summertime	l'heure d'été (f.)	*luhr daytay*
sun	le soleil	*luh solehy*
sun hat	le chapeau de soleil/ le bonnet	*luh shahpoa duh solehy/ luh boneh*
sunbathe	prendre un bain de soleil	*prohndr uhn bahn duh solehy*
sunburn	le coup de soleil	*luh koo duh solehy*
Sunday	dimanche	*deemohnsh*
sunglasses	les lunettes de soleil	*lay lewneht duh solehy*
sunrise	le lever du soleil	*luh luhvay duh solehy*
sunset	le coucher du soleil	*luh kooshay duh solehy*
suntan lotion	la crème solaire	*lah krehm solehr*
suntan oil	l'huile solaire (f.)	*lweel sohlehr*
supermarket	le supermarché	*luh sewpehrmahrshay*
surcharge	le supplément	*luh sewplaymohn*
surf board	la planche à voile	*lah plohnsh ah vwahl*
surgery	la consultation	*lah kawnsewltahsyawn*
surname	le nom	*luh nawn*
surprise	la surprise	*lah sewrpreez*
swallow	avaler	*ahvahlay*
swamp	le marais	*luh mahreh*
sweat	la transpiration	*lah trohnspeerahsyawn*
sweet	le bonbon	*luh bawnbawn*
sweet (kind)	gentil	*jhohntee*
sweet (adj.)	sucré	*sewkray*
sweetcorn	le maïs	*luh mahees*
sweets	les friandises	*lay freeohndeez*
swim	nager	*nahjhay*
swimming pool	la piscine	*lah peeseen*
swimming trunks	le maillot de bain	*luh mahyoa duh bahn*
swindle	l'escroquerie (f.)	*lehskrokree*
switch	l'interrupteur (m.)	*lahntayrewptuhr*
synagogue	la synagogue	*lah seenahgog*

table	la table	*lah tahbl*
table tennis	jouer au ping-pong	*jhooay oa peeng pawng*
tablet	le comprimé	*luh kawnpreemay*
take (use)	utiliser	*ewteeleezay*
take	prendre	*prohndr*
take (time)	durer	*dewray*
take pictures	photographier	*foatoagrahfyay*
taken	occupé	*okewpay*
talcum powder	le talc	*luh tahlk*
talk	parler	*pahrlay*
tall	grand	*grohn*
tampons	les tampons	*lay tohnpawn*
tanned	brun	*bruhn*
tap	le robinet	*luh robeeneh*
tap water	l'eau du robinet (f.)	*loa dew robeeneh*
tartlet	la tartelette	*lah tahrtuhleht*
taste	goûter	*gootay*
tax free shop	le magasin hors-taxes	*luh mahgahzahn or tahx*
taxi	le taxi	*luh tahxee*
taxi stand	la station de taxis	*lah stahsyawn duh tahxee*
tea	le thé	*luh tay*
teapot	la théière	*lah tay-yehr*
teaspoon	la petite cuillère	*lah puhteet kweeyehr*
telephoto lens	le téléobjectif	*luh taylayobjhehkteef*
television	la télévision	*lah taylayveezyawn*
temperature	la température	*lah tohnpayrahtewr*
temporary filling	le plombage provisoire	*luh plawnbahjh proveezwahr*
tender	tendre	*tohndr*
tennis (play)	jouer au tennis	*jhooay oa taynees*
tennis ball	la balle de tennis	*lah bahl duh taynees*
tennis court	le court de tennis	*luh koor duh taynees*
tennis racket	la raquette de tennis	*lah rahkeht duh taynees*
tent	la tente	*lah tohnt*
tent peg	le piquet	*luh peekay*

errace	la terrasse	*lah tehrahs*
errible	épouvantable	*aypoovohntahbl*
hank	remercier	*ruhmehrsyay*
hank you	merci bien	*mehrsee byahn*
hanks	merci	*mehrsee*
haw	dégeler	*dayjhuhlay*
heatre	le théâtre	*luh tayahtr*
heft	le vol	*luh vol*
here	là	*lah*
hermal bath	le bain thermal	*luh bahn tehrmahl*
hermometer	le thermomètre	*luh tehrmomehtr*
hick	gros	*groa*
hief	le voleur	*luh voluhr*
high	la cuisse	*lah kwees*
hin	maigre	*mehgr*
hink	penser	*pohnsay*
hird	le tiers	*luh tyehr*
hirsty, to be	la soif	*lah swahf*
his afternoon	cet après-midi	*seht ahpreh meedee*
his evening	ce soir	*suh swahr*
his morning	ce matin	*suh mahtahn*
hread	le fil	*luh feel*
hroat	la gorge	*lah gorjh*
hroat lozenges	les pastilles pour la gorge	*lay pahsteey poor lah gorjh*
hrow up	vomir	*vomeer*
hunderstorm	l'orage (m.)	*lorajh*
hursday	jeudi	*jhuhdee*
cket (admission)	le billet	*luh beeyeh*
cket (travel)	le ticket	*luh teekeh*
dy	ranger	*rohnjhay*
e	la cravate	*lah krahvaht*
ghts	le collant	*luh kolohn*
me (clock)	l'heure (f.)	*luhr*
me (occasion)	la fois	*lah fwah*
metable	l'horaire des arrivées et des départs	*lorehr day zahreevay ay day daypahr*
n	la boîte de conserve	*lah bwaht duh kawnsehrv*

tip	le pourboire	*luh poorbwahr*
tissues	les mouchoirs en papier	*lay mooshwahr ohn pahpyay*
toast	le toast	*luh toast*
tobacco	le tabac	*luh tahbah*
toboggan	la luge	*lah lewjh*
today	aujourd'hui	*oajhoordwee*
toe	l'orteil (m.)	*lortehy*
together	ensemble	*ohnsohnbl*
toilet	les toilettes	*lay twahleht*
toilet paper	le papier hygiénique	*luh pahpyay eejhyayneek*
toiletries	les articles de toilette	*lay zahrteekl duh twahleht*
tomato	la tomate	*lah tomaht*
tomato purée	le concentré de tomates	*luh kawnsohntray duh tomaht*
tomato sauce	le ketchup	*luh kehtchuhp*
tomorrow	demain	*duhmahn*
tongue	la langue	*lah lohng*
tonic water	le tonic	*luh toneek*
tonight	ce soir	*suh swahr*
tonight	cette nuit	*seht nwee*
too much	trop	*troa*
tools	les outils	*lay zootee*
tooth	la dent	*lah dohn*
toothache	le mal de dents	*luh mahl duh dohn*
toothbrush	la brosse à dents	*lah bros ah dohn*
toothpaste	le dentifrice	*luh dohnteefrees*
toothpick	le cure-dent	*luh kewrdohn*
top up	remplir	*rohnpleer*
total	le total	*luh totahl*
tough	dur	*dewr*
tour	le tour	*luh toor*
tour guide	le guide	*luh geed*
tourist card	la carte touristique	*lah kahrt tooreesteek*
tourist class	la classe touriste	*lah klahs tooreest*
Tourist Information	l'office de tourisme office	*lofees duh tooreesm office*
tow	remorquer	*ruhmorkay*

ow cable	le câble	*luh kahbl*
owel	la serviette de toilette	*lah sehrvyeht duh twahleht*
ower	la tour	*lah toor*
own	la ville	*lah veel*
own hall	la mairie	*lah mayree*
oy	le jouet	*luh jhooeh*
raffic	la circulation	*lah seerkewlahsyawn*
raffic light	le feu de signalisation	*luh fuh duh seenyahleezahsyawn*
rain	le train	*luh trahn*
rain ticket	le billet de train	*luh beeyeh duh trahn*
rain timetable	l'indicateur des chemins de fer	*lahndeekahtuhr day shuhmahn duh fehr*
ranslate	traduire	*trahdweer*
avel	voyager	*vwahyahjhay*
avel agent	l'agence de voyages (f.)	*lahjhohns duh vwahyahjh*
avel guide	le guide touristique	*luh geed tooreesteek*
aveller	le voyageur	*luh vwahyahjhuhr*
aveller's cheque	le chèque de voyage	*luh shehk duh vwahyahjh*
eacle	la mélasse	*lah maylahs*
eatment	le traitement	*luh trehtmohn*
iangle	le triangle	*luh treeohngl*
im	tailler	*tahy-yay*
ip	l'excursion (f.)/ le voyage	*lehxkewrsyawn/ luh vwahyahjh*
out	la truite	*lah trweet*
unk call	interurbain	*ahntehrewrbahn*
unk code	l'indicatif (m.)	*lahndeekahteef*
ustworthy	de confiance	*duh kawnfyohns*
y on	essayer	*ehsay-yay*
ibe	le tube	*luh tewb*
uesday	mardi	*mahrdee*
umble drier	le sèche-linge	*luh sahsh lahnjh*
una	le thon	*luh tawn*
unnel	le tunnel	*luh tewnehl*
v	la télé	*lah taylay*
veezers	la pince	*lah pahns*

tyre	le pneu	*luh pnuh*
tyre lever	le démonte-pneu	*luh daymawnt pnuh*
tyre pressure	la pression des pneus	*lah prehsyawn day pnuh*

U

ugly	laid	*leh*
umbrella	le parapluie	*luh pahrahplwee*
under	sous	*soo*
underground (train)	le métro	*luh maytroa*
underground	le réseau	*luh rayzoa*
railway system	métropolitain	*maytroapoleetahn*
underground station	la station de métro	*lah stahsyawn duh maytroa*
underpants	le slip	*luh sleep*
understand	comprendre	*kawnprohndr*
underwear	les sous-vêtements	*lay soovehtmohn*
undress	(se) déshabiller	*suh dayzahbeeyay*
unemployed	au chômage	*oa shoamahjh*
uneven	irrégulier	*eeraygewlyay*
university	l'université (f.)	*lewneevehrseetay*
unleaded	sans plomb	*sohn plawn*
up	en haut	*ohn oa*
urgent	urgent	*ewrjhohn*
urine	l'urine (f.)	*lewreen*
usually	généralement	*jhaynayrahlmohn*

V

vacate	évacuer	*ayvahkeway*
vaccinate	vacciner	*vahkseenay*
vagina	le vagin	*luh vahjhahn*
vaginal infection	l'infection vaginale	*lahnfehksyawn vahjheenahl*
valid	valable	*vahlahbl*
valley	la vallée	*lah vahlay*

an	la camionnette	*lah kahmyoneht*
anilla	la vanille	*lah vahneey*
ase	le vase	*luh vahz*
aseline	la vaseline	*lah vahzleen*
eal	la viande de veau	*lah vyohnd duh voa*
egetable soup	la soupe de légumes	*lah soop duh laygewm*
egetables	le légume	*luh laygewm*
egetarian	le végétarien	*luh vayjhaytahryahn*
ein	la veine	*lah vehn*
ending machine	le distributeur	*luh deestreebewtuhr*
enereal disease	la maladie vénérienne	*lah mahlahdee vaynayryehn*
ia	par	*pahr*
ideo recorder	le magnétoscope	*luh manyehtoskop*
iew	la vue	*lah vew*
illage	le village	*luh veelahjh*
isa	le visa	*luh veezah*
isit (verb)	rendre visite à	*rohndr veezeet ah*
isit	la visite	*lah veezeet*
tamin	la vitamine	*lah veetahmeen*
tamin tablet	le comprimé de vitamines	*luh kawnpreemay duh veetahmeen*
olcano	le volcan	*luh volkohn*
olleyball	jouer au volley	*jhooay oa volay*
omit	vomir	*vomeer*

W

ait	attendre	*ahtohndr*
aiter	le serveur	*luh sehrvuhr*
aiting room	la salle d'attente	*lah sahl dahtohnt*
aitress	la serveuse	*lah sehrvuhz*
ake up	réveiller	*rayvay-yay*
alk	la promenade	*lah promnahd*
alk (verb)	se promener/marcher	*suh promnay/mahrshay*
allet	le portefeuille	*luh portuhfuhy*
ardrobe	la garde-robe	*lah gahrd rob*

warm	chaud	*shoa*
warn	prévenir	*prayvuhneer*
warning	l'avertissement (m.)	*lahvehrteesmohn*
wash	laver	*lahvay*
washing-powder	le détergent	*luh daytehrjhohn*
washing	le linge	*luh lahnjh*
washing line	la corde à linge	*lah kord ah lahnjh*
washing machine	la machine à laver	*lah mahsheen ah lahvay*
wasp	la guêpe	*lah gehp*
water	l'eau (f.)	*loa*
water ski	faire du ski nautique	*fehr dew skee noateek*
waterproof	imperméable	*ahnpehrmayahbl*
wave-pool	la piscine à vagues artificielles	*lah peeseen ah vahg zahrteefeesyehl*
way	le moyen/ la direction	*luh mwahyahn/ lah deerehksyawn*
we	nous	*noo*
weak	faible	*fehbl*
weather	le temps	*luh tohn*
weather forecast	le bulletin météorologique	*luh bewltahn maytayoarolojheek*
wedding	les noces/le mariage	*lay nos/luh mahryajh*
Wednesday	mercredi	*mehrkruhdee*
week	la semaine	*lah suhmehn*
weekend	le week-end	*luh week-ehnd*
weekend duty	le service de garde	*luh sehrvees duh gahrd*
weekly ticket	l'abonnement hebdomadaire (m.)	*lahbonmohn ehbdomahdehr*
welcome	bienvenu	*byahnvuhnew*
well	bien	*byahn*
west	l'ouest (m.)	*lwehst*
wet	humide	*ewmeed*
wetsuit	la combinaison de planche à voile	*lah kawnbeenehzawn duh plohnsh ah vwahl*
what?	quoi?	*kwah?*
wheel	la roue	*lah roo*
wheelchair	la chaise roulante	*lah shehz roolohnt*

when?	quand?	*kohn?*
where?	où?	*oo?*
which?	quel?	*kehl?*
whipped cream	la crème Chantilly	*lah krehm shohnteeyee*
white	blanc	*blohn*
who?	qui?	*kee?*
wholemeal bread	le pain complet	*luh pahn kawnpleh*
why?	pourquoi?	*poorkwah?*
wide-angle lens	le grand-angle	*luh grohn tohngl*
widow	la veuve	*lah vuhv*
widower	le veuf	*luh vuhf*
wife	l'épouse (f.)	*laypooz*
wind	le vent	*luh vohn*
windbreak	le pare-vent	*luh pahrvohn*
windmill	le moulin	*luh moolahn*
window (desk)	le guichet	*luh gueesheh*
window	la fenêtre	*lah fuhnehtr*
windscreen wiper	l'essuie-glace (m.)	*lehswee glahs*
windsurf	faire de la planche à voile	*fehr duh lah plohnsh ah vwahl*
wine	le vin	*luh vahn*
wine list	la carte des vins	*lah kahrt day vahn*
winter	l'hiver (m.)	*leevehr*
witness	le témoin	*luh taymwahn*
woman	la femme	*lah fahm*
wood	le bois	*luh bwah*
wool	la laine	*lah lehn*
word	le mot	*luh moa*
work	le travail	*luh trahvahy*
working day	le jour ouvrable	*jhoor oovrahbl*
worn	usé	*ewzay*
worried	inquiet	*ahnkyeh*
wound	la blessure	*lah blehsewr*
wrap	emballer	*ohnbahlay*
wrist	le poignet	*luh pwahnnyeh*
write	écrire	*aykreer*
write down	noter	*notay*

writing pad	le bloc-notes	*luh blok not*
writing paper	le papier à lettres	*luh pahpyay ah lehtr*
written	écrit	*aykree*
wrong	mauvais	*moaveh*

Y

yacht	le yacht	*luh yot*
year	l'année (f.)	*lahnay*
yellow	jaune	*jhoan*
yes	oui	*wee*
yes, please	volontiers	*volawntyay*
yesterday	hier	*yehr*
yoghurt	le yaourt	*luh yahoort*
you	vous	*voo*
you too	de même	*duh mehm*
youth hostel	l'auberge de jeunesse (f.)	*loabehrjh duh jhuhnehs*

Z

| zip | la fermeture éclair | *lah fehrmuhtewr ayklehr* |
| zoo | le parc zoologique | *luh pahrk zoaolojheek* |